INDIE AUTHOR MAGAZINE

HELLO AND WELCOME!

I'm Indie Annie, and I'm thrilled you're reading this gorgeous full-color version of IAM. Did you know that you can also access all the information, education, and inspiration in our app? It's available on both the iOS App Store and Google Play. And for those that prefer to listen to me read articles, you can pop over to Spotify or our website.

Happy Reading!

X

IndieAuthorMagazine.com

Betas and ARCs

INDIE AUTHOR MAGAZINE
Betas & ARCs
Your Biggest ARC Team Questions, Answered
10 Tips for Better Beta Reader Feedback
A Journalist's Guide to the Perfect Press Release
The Reader Magnet Revolution
Authenticity and Buzz: A Closer Look at What Beta Readers and ARC Readers Have to Offer
A Thousand Li: The Second Sect
Book 3
Volume 2 • Issue 6 • June 2022
This Issue's Featured Author:
Tao Wong

ON THE COVER

PUBLISHER
Athenia Creative
6820 Apus Dr.
Sparks, NV, 89436 USA
775.298.1925

ISSN 2768-7880 (online)–ISSN 2768-7872 (print)

From the Publisher

UPGRADE YOUR BRAIN'S OPERATING SYSTEM

I have a new analogy I'd like to share this month. Indulge me as I rock this newborn while her exhausted parents try to get a nap.

When you become a grandparent, the universe upgrades your operating system with a new app called "Been There Done That."

It pulls the most obscure memories out of your brain's deep freeze related to how you did things with your kids. You're now able to confidently say, "Oh, yes, that's normal. You did that," or, "Hmm ... I went through that with your sister. The urge to scream will pass. Hang in there."

Voila! You managed to keep them alive, so now you're an expert on all things parenting. You're wise. Seasoned. *You know things.*

When we pursue a career as an indie author, we're like new parents. We don't know anything, and it seems as overwhelming as a 3:00 a.m. feeding with a screaming baby.

Luckily, this is a generous industry, with a lot of folks who have the "Been There Done That" app installed. They're ready and willing to share their stories of what worked and what didn't so no one has to go it alone.

You're learning and growing. Every new thing brings more knowledge.

You'll find a lot of that wisdom tucked into every article. Soak it up. You'll find your brain's operating system upgraded in no time as you too start to know things. Then you'll be able to help another indie on their journey.

To Your Success,

Chelle
Publisher
Indie Author Magazine

AUTHOR·TECH·SUMMIT

Begins: August 30, 2022

AuthorTechSummit.com

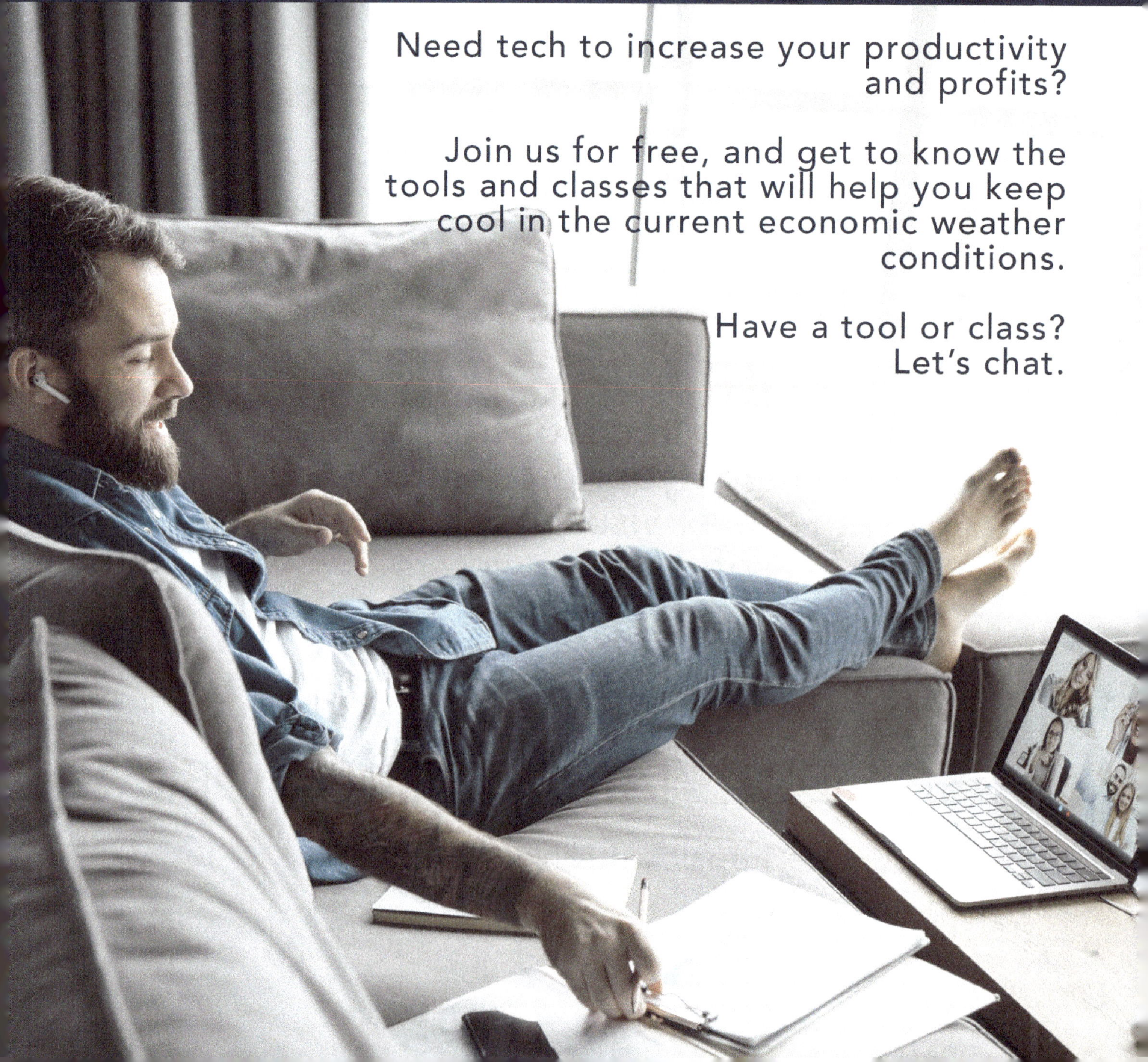

Believe You Can, and You Will

You didn't write your book by accident, and your author career won't take off by mistake.

It starts with you.

If you don't believe in yourself, how will others believe in you? Flip that switch and know that you are doing the best you can, doing better today than yesterday. What is the value of that?

If you feel you can do it, you can. And then after you've done it, you'll wonder why you ever doubted yourself, just until you second guess yourself all over again.

It's not luck. It takes the determination of hours at the keyboard. It takes reading. It takes re-reading what you wrote—sometimes that's the hardest part. But it shows your mettle, your tenacity.

You fix your words and move on.

How many people have you heard say they wanted to write a book? How many have? You're not comparing yourself to them but to yourself. You set out to write a book, and you did. You lived up to your word.

That deserves a celebration. That is an elite level of success. Then you sell your book to strangers. That's your next level, the next step up the mountain of success.

No one is born an expert. It takes practice and dedication. It may seem like one person seems to have more innate storytelling talent than another. I would chalk that up to reading, always reading stories and analyzing, "What if?" What would make my story different? What holds my attention?

And then you try, and your story doesn't look anything like the one that inspired you.

Of course not. Your first effort can't be compared with someone else's lifetime achievement. Your stories can only be compared with yours.

The readers serve as the final arbiters. They will be hard, but they will be forgiving if you've delivered a good story, even if it could have been written better.

Do that. Write the next one better. Practice. Read. Learn. And write some more.

Believe in yourself, and others will come to believe too. ■

Craig Martelle

Dear Indie Annie,

I'm dyslexic, and my family says I should focus my creative energies on arts like pottery, but in my heart, I know I want to write. Are there any other dyslexic writers out there?

Dyslexic in Dysart

DEAR . . .?

You know, often people label themselves as Frustrated from Fairbanks or whatever, and regular fans of my humble missives will know that I often change their names before we begin. And I feel on this occasion, darling Dyslexic in Dysart, that there has never been a greater need than now to challenge your label.

Dyslexia is more than an inability to read like a mainstream neurotypical (NT) person. Dyslexia, dysgraphia, and dyscalculia offer the world an alternate viewpoint. And my sweet Discoverer in Dysart, isn't that the very essence of being a writer? The ability to reimagine, to see the world through a different lens.

Your family has spotted that you are creative. Of course they have. People with neurodiverse filters are a veritable cornucopia of great ideas and fascinating concepts and constructs that serve to enrich the world for the rest of us. And that is all you have: a different, beautifully creative filter on the world.

Instead of seeing this as an obstacle, think of it as a superpower. Now you need to assemble a team or a fancy utility belt around you to maximize that superpower—even the Avengers couldn't do it alone.

So what do you need?

When I quickly googled Marvel for this response, the official site came back with a glossary of 2,631 characters—2,631! Each one had their own offering to the universe and their own adaptations to normal life.

Equally, not all dyslexics are the same. You may also present with signs of ADHD or other diagnoses. Superheroes come in all shapes and sizes and have adapted accordingly—not only to operate more efficiently in a non-superhero world but also to maximize their particular talents.

I'm going to mix up my DC and Marvel characters here, but heading over to DC Comics, let's explore two classics that have been reimagined over and over again—Batman and Superman. Superman

Need help from your favorite Indie Aunt?
Ask Dear Indie Annie a question at
IndieAnnie@indieauthormagazine.com

struggles to fit in as Clark Kent, hiding his abilities until he passes a handy phone box. Bruce Wayne has no superhuman gift but has used his enormous wealth to create a range of tools in his lair to call into action whenever Gotham sends up the Bat-Signal across the sky. You do what you have to do to save the world, right?

I presume you have had a formal assessment and diagnosis. You will, therefore, already have a handle on what tips and techniques can help guide you through this neurotypical world. But could you try new strategies or find people to ask for help?

Are you a Batman? Do you need to build yourself a lair filled with cutting-edge technology? I am thinking of digital platforms with nifty algorithms that will help you improve your writing. Scrivener may help you organize all your creative thoughts in one place with tools to rearrange and order them in a way that works for you. Software like Grammarly and ProWritingAid will help flag spelling, grammatical, and syntax errors. Dragon can capture your spoken word, and text-to-speech apps will help you if you think better using auditory tools. Pinterest is great to help you visualize. Mind-mapping tools can help you create a web of random interconnectedness that Spider-Man would be proud of. I could go on, but like Superman, I am needed back at the day job, and my outerwear is giving me a wedgie.

I suggest you review past issues of this illustrious publication and check out their suggestions.

If you are more of a Marvel fan, then you need to assemble your Avengers. Ask neurotypical friends and family to read your drafts and edit/proofread your work in progress before submitting to an editor.

One tip I read somewhere was to write in Comic Sans. Personally, I really miss that font. It used to be ubiquitous but is now the social outcast of the font community. Try it out—it's supposed to work wonders for people with dyslexia. Just remember to convert back to something boring like Times New Roman or Ariel before you send your work out into the world, or people will think you are the Joker!

Oh, and dear Discoverer, as to the final part of your question: Are there any other dyslexic writers? Of course there are. You might recognize a few of these creative names: F. Scott Fitzgerald, Agatha Christie, WB Yeats, Gustave Flaubert, George Bernard Shaw, John Irving, Sally Gardner, Patricia Polacco, Ahmet Zappa, and Jules Verne.

Happy writing,
Indie Annie

10 TIPS FOR
BETTER BETA READER FEEDBACK

You've finally written "The End," and it's now time for the next stage in prepping your manuscript for publication: Find some beta readers who will take your story and help you make it better.

But what's a beta reader, where do you find these mythical beings, and how can you make the most of them?

Read on! You know we've got you covered.

WHAT IS A BETA READER?

Beta readers will read your book and give you helpful feedback on it. But you want more than just "I liked it" or "Yes, it was good." That's great for the ego, but it doesn't tell you anything about how to improve your book.

You want people who will take the time to carefully read your story and make notes on what did and didn't work for them. Beta readers look at your story with fresh eyes, and they will pick up on issues you missed simply because you're too close to the story.

1 FIND YOUR BETA READERS

You can easily search Facebook and Goodreads for groups where you can ask for beta readers. You can also ask your writer friends where they've found theirs, post in genre-specific groups if allowed, and ask in your own reader group.

Should you pay for beta readers? Well, like much in the indie author world, it depends. Most of the time, you won't pay for beta readers, but you may need to if you need a specialist, such as if you're writing a police procedural and need an expert who can make sure your writing is correct. You might also consider paying a professional if you just haven't got the time to go through the process of finding your own or if you want to be sure of the quality of your reader. Costs vary for hired beta readers from just a few dollars to around 300 to 400 dollars.

Pro Tip: Use software to manage your beta readers. Sites such as BetaReader (https://betareader.io/) and BetaBooks (https://betabooks.co/) let you manage your beta readers and easily collate your feedback.

2 ASSESS YOUR TEAM

It's great when you get a lot of volunteers to beta your story; however, you need reliable people who will stick to your deadline and do the work. When you're looking for beta readers, ask them questions and find out if they have any experience. A lack of experience doesn't rule them out, but at least find out if they know what's involved and how long it might take them.

Make sure they are a fan of your genre too. There's no point in asking someone who hates fantasy and zombie stories to read your fantasy romance spin on *The Walking Dead*. All that will give you is endless criticism that you don't need.

Check if they are a writer. You will get different feedback from someone who also writes rather than someone who only reads. This can be great as they know what you're looking for, but they may also comment on how you can fix your story, which may not be what you want.

3 KEEP THE NUMBER MANAGEABLE

Three to five readers per round is a solid number as it's enough for different opinions but not so many that you'll be overwhelmed. You'll be able to establish any patterns and find areas that most of your readers agree on. And with an odd number, you also have a tie-breaker vote if you're unsure what to do with a piece of feedback.

As for how many rounds you need, well, that's up to you. Do as many rounds as you think is necessary to improve the story.

Pro Tip: Send your story out to beta readers in batches, not all at once. You'll want someone new to assess the changes you've made after the first round of beta readers so you can see if you've solved the problem. This ensures that every version of your story that's been beta read and self-edited has had at least another pair of eyes before your book goes to your editor.

4 PROVIDE A CLEAN DRAFT

Your beta readers are looking for big picture issues, not spelling mistakes and punctuation. If you provide an error-riddled draft, they'll probably get distracted by that, and they may miss weak spots you really needed to know.

Make it easy on them. They're doing you a favor, so give them their copy in the format they want as long as it has the option for them to add comments. Microsoft Word works well since most people have it and you can track changes, but you may need to print and post copies to beta readers who prefer to hold a copy in their hand.

5 ADD TRIGGER WARNINGS

Many people have topics that they can't read about without getting upset. Even if it's only a tiny paragraph halfway down page thirty, make sure you warn people up front that your writing may deal with uncomfortable, disturbing, or triggering topics. Don't give your helpful beta readers a negative experience. They might not come back.

6 GIVE CLEAR INSTRUCTIONS

Give your beta readers a clear deadline that gives you plenty of time to incorporate their feedback. Give them at least a couple of weeks to get through your book. Let them know you will be checking in with them part of the way through to make sure they're okay and can finish on time. If you don't check in until the due date, they may have forgotten about your story, and then you will have no time to get any feedback from elsewhere.

Tell them what you're looking for and give them questions to answer, such as:

- Does the opening grab you?
- Would you read on after the end of each chapter?
- Is anything unclear?
- Does the story flow?
- What do you think of X or Y characters?

Don't overwhelm them, but the clearer you are in your expectations, the better feedback you'll get.

7 MANAGE YOUR EXPECTATIONS

You may be lucky enough to find an amazing beta reader who basically does a full developmental edit for you, but you can't expect that. Beta readers are there to catch specific issues that you're looking for, not to save you the cost of an editor.

8 PUT ON YOUR BIG GIRL PANTIES

It's never easy taking criticism, even if it's well meant and genuinely helpful. We get it. But you'll never improve or see your blind spots without your lovely beta readers, so buckle up!

Try to keep in mind that these people really do want to help you and that they're not being deliberately mean or trying to make you feel bad.

9 TAKE WHAT YOU NEED FROM IT

However, you don't have to accept all the feedback. You are allowed to make the final decision about what you keep and what you ignore.

Take the time to go through your comments and decide what you'll implement and what you'll reject. But be careful of knee-jerk reactions. We get that you're attached to all your characters and that you loved writing that particular scene, but if it isn't working for your beta readers, take a step back and do your best to be objective.

ORGANIZE AND APPLY YOUR FEEDBACK

Wait until you have feedback from all your beta readers before you start applying it. You can then organize it properly and compare each person's feedback.

You'll probably end up with three types of feedback: feedback you ignore, feedback that you use, and feedback you're not sure of.

Put the ignore pile in a separate document so it's there if you want it, but you don't have to pay any attention to it if you don't want to.

Then look at your unsure pile. Go through this again, but don't spend too much time on it. Quickly use your instincts to mark each piece of advice either as something to ignore or to use, then move what you don't want to your ignore document.

Collate your helpful feedback so it's ready for implementation, and organize it in an order that makes sense for how you'll edit your story.

Then just go through and make the changes you know will make your story shine.

Pro Tip: Say "thank you!" Your beta readers really can be the difference between a dull draft that costs you a ton of extra money on edits and a shiny, polished draft that flies through edits. Tell them often how much you appreciate them. Consider sending them goodies, such as swag, and a free signed copy of the print book when it's complete. You'll develop a great relationship that will benefit you both. ■

Gill Fernley

Making Money Moves

TAO WONG SHARES HIS SECRETS FOR MAKING THE FULL-TIME GIG WORK FINANCIALLY

> I write heroes, partly because I believe we need more of them in our world.
> -Tao Wong

Tao Wong never meant to be a full-time author. Now he helps other authors move closer to realizing the same dream he never thought he'd achieve, all while advocating the necessity of income diversification.

His backlist speaks for itself. Tao currently has more than five series, though he is probably best known for his Post-apocalyptic LitRPG series, The System Apocalypse, and his Chinese Xianxia Fantasy series, A Thousand Li. His book, *A Thousand Li: The Second Sect* was short-listed for the UK Kindle Storyteller in 2021. Xianxia Fantasy, also sometimes referred to as Cultivation Fantasy, is a martial arts novel genre heavily influenced by Chinese mythology—on his website (https://MyLifeMyTao.com), Tao describes it as something akin to "Eastern Fantasy."

Tao credits his early success to the fact that he published "at a time when LitRPG was very much in demand at Amazon, and people found my work and enjoyed reading it."

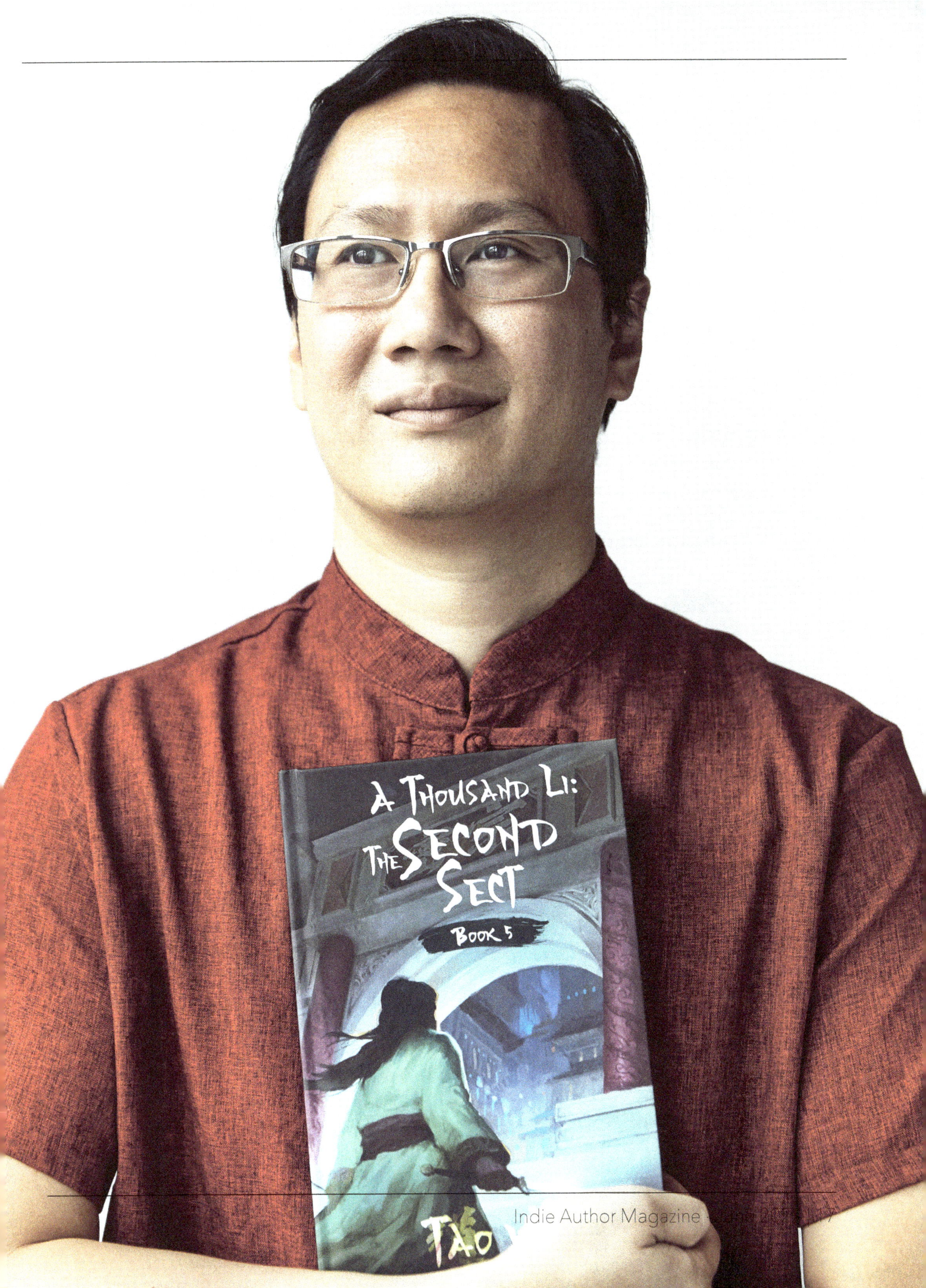
A Thousand Li:
The Second Sect
Book 5
Tao

Asked what he thinks makes a good story, Tao replied that "hitting the tropes of whatever genre you're writing in" will help you connect with your readership. Personally, he says he writes characters who are like himself but slightly different. A common theme in his books is "the price of choices"—often, his characters are forced to grapple with the consequences of decisions they've made.

"I write heroes, partly because I believe we need more of them in our world. But also, the choices that we make, and the decisions that we make, knowing that there is a consequence to all of these decisions … is important to learn and to write about," Tao says.

LOOK BEFORE YOU LEAP

When it comes to writing, Tao says it took him five years to figure out he was a "plantser"—not creating an outline for his books in the traditional sense, but not necessarily diving in without a plan either. "I have a beginning and an end," he says, but he doesn't plot out what happens in between. The characters take the story and run with it. He's also tried discovery writing, in which he didn't know what the ending would be, but he found it wasted time, and he would consistently have to cut thousands of words from his final manuscript.

On the business side of authorship, Tao waited before he started advertising. "For the first two years, all I did was write, publish, write, publish," Tao says. After building a steady backlist with about five books in each series, Tao dived into Facebook advertising and AMS ads. He's a firm believer that an author shouldn't advertise or push a book too soon because it doesn't get a solid return on investment. He advocates having the marketing platform of a website and a newsletter, but he believes an author's focus should be on writing.

When it comes to giving guidance to authors hoping to go full

time, "make sure you have a backlist," Tao says. His second piece of advice is practical: Make sure your minimum income suffices to handle your bills. He didn't go full time until the lowest month of earnings in the previous year was enough to settle his bills. For himself, Tao needed to ensure he had sufficient funds to cover all his costs. He admits that he could have gone full time a little earlier, but he had a secondary business, an e-commerce game retailer, he had to wind down first. He recommends creators have at least six months of savings before making the leap, though he prefers a year's worth of funds to cover expenses and savings. "Running a business is generally more expensive than you will ever expect, and it's hard to know how much it's going to cost until you've done it a couple of years running," Tao says.

Authors should also account for the transition from part-time to full-time status. He shares that everyone thinks they will get more words down when they go full time, but it's difficult to do. More time does not necessarily equate to more words.

BRANCHING OUT

As a savvy businessman and author, Tao emphasizes diversifying sources of income. "It plays a big part in determining your business and marketing strat-

egies, not just in the sheer volume of processes needed but also the kinds of audiences you touch," he says. He insists that "diversification and income streams is risk management" that every author should take into account.

Tao learned the necessity for income diversification the hard way with his previous venture, Starlit Citadel. One of the income streams for his e-commerce business was Amazon, and it shut his seller account down without cause for three months until the company eventually reinstated it. "If we weren't diversified, that would have destroyed us," he says. It's the reason he's keen to ensure he has multiple revenue streams.

At the moment, Tao makes a large percentage of his earnings from Kindle Unlimited and Audible, but he always looks for ways to diversify his cash flow because he doesn't want to be in a position where he has zero revenue.

A visit to his website, MyLifeMyTao.com, shows multiple business posts teaching authors how to grow the potential of their intellectual property. Authors can channel a novel through various touchpoints in a pipeline designed to maximize reach and earnings.

Tao uses Patreon, Kickstarter, and direct sales from his website to supplement the compensation he generates from Amazon. There are multiple benefits of extending the book publication pipeline, he says, such as rewards for readers, the ability to have stress-free deadlines, and consistently generated income.

> Having a good story is the first step to success.

Patreon

Tao explains that he's able to write a clean initial draft, and as a result, "Patreon gets my first draft immediately as I write it." This pleases his most ardent fans, desperate to read the next book in the series. Offering loyal readers the opportunity to get an early look at chapters as he finishes them builds stronger bonds besides providing a steady income.

Kickstarter

Eventually, Tao plans to add Kickstarter as another marketing tool in his wheelhouse, mainly because readers on Kickstarter are different from the Amazon audience. It's also "a way of touching the wide readership" and expanding his income stream, he says, since his books are usually exclusively in Kindle Unlimited. Kickstarter backers would get the first version of the novel after the chapters are edited.

Direct Sales Through His Website

The third touchstone, Tao's publishing company, Starlit Publishing, allows readers to buy a book directly from him without having to go through Kickstarter. The various funnels in the pipeline allow Tao to touch upon different audiences, a method of expanding his readership.

Amazon

A couple of months after distributing a new novel directly, Tao publishes it on Amazon, and his Kindle Unlimited readership is able to consume the book through the retailer.

Some of this pipeline resulted from Tao's realization that he was pushing himself too hard and falling behind on releases, having to rush because he had editors, proofreaders, narrators, and other people he'd contracted who were waiting for his manuscript. The updated publishing timeline relieves the stress of hitting deadlines by extending his time frame for creating a final product, all while allowing him to continue generating revenue.

A WORD TO THE WISE

Another mode of income diversification resulted in Tao branching into co-authoring projects. He approached others to write in his worlds. Asked about his process, Tao admits the relationship differs with each co-author; however, in most cases, he comes in afterward as a developmental editor. There is "a lot of communication involved," he says, but "co-authoring is another avenue of splitting income, working with new people, helping some [authors] up, and improving your craft."

Early in 2021, Tao ran a grant offering one writer a chance to get up to two thousand dollars to put toward their publishing goals. He says he believes in giving back to the community and extending a supporting hand to authors. In the future, he hopes to offer more people the opportunity by increasing the number of grants.

"We talk a lot about the business side," Tao says. "We need to be working on our craft, and that is a continuous thing." After all, having a good story is the first step to success. ■

Fatima Fayez

Authenticity and Buzz

A CLOSER LOOK AT WHAT BETA READERS AND ARC READERS HAVE TO OFFER

If you already swap chapters with author friends, you know what it's like to have critique partners. But have you considered beta readers to deepen your storytelling or ARC [advanced reader copy] readers to create pre-release buzz about your amazing new book?

First, let's make sure we keep our expert readers straight. The difference between critique partners, beta readers, and ARC readers is their proximity to your target audience. Critique partners have "writer brains." They probably can't resist brilliant suggestions for improving your work-in-progress. In contrast, a beta reader reads your target genre and understands that you need honest—but not nasty!—feedback to create your best work. They point out their reactions and possible problems but not solutions.

"Beta reads are typically done after the manuscript is 'finished' (we all know that varies), so the author can get a sense of how someone who knows little to nothing about the story enjoys the book. It's testing the book to see if it's ready to go," writes Janice Hardy, author and founder of Fiction University website. "The goal of a beta reader is to read the novel as if they'd purchased it and essentially give the author 'a review' of the book from the general reader perspective."

While beta readers give a private review directly to the author, ARC readers share their reading experience with the public. An ARC reader focuses on serving your future readers with a public review of your book—their work isn't for you.

WHEN MIGHT BETA READERS FIT INTO YOUR PRODUCTION PLANS?

Once you have your manuscript together, it becomes a prototype. A beta reader is the perfect person to take your proto-book for a test drive.

The best beta readers have "reader brains" and report on their experience, not on your technique or mistakes. By designing a concise questionnaire for your beta readers, you have a chance to put on your sports commentator badge and ask, "Now that the journey's over, how are you feeling?" A beta reader gives you the inside story on your story. Your job is then to figure out what to do with that feedback—what to fix and how to fix it.

That's why the authors on the March 17 episode of the Fully

Booked podcast recommend a small number of beta readers—three or five for tie-breaking purposes. "Five's my maximum," says author Helen Yeomans. "They're so much work."

Feedback from beta readers means intensive detective work for you. You need to figure out what made the reader bored, confused, or frustrated. The solution might be in another chapter or a motivation problem instead of a plot problem. This is a major difference between a beta reader and an editor: A beta reader will tell you what the problem is while an editor will also tell you how to fix it.

Here are a few key signs it's time to book a beta read for your manuscript.

Your book is aimed at a new audience, or you are branching out into a new genre.

Beta readers can tell you if their expectations were met for the tropes in your targeted genre or give you hints that you've actually written something else. No shame in that. But it's much easier to market a book if you know what genre it is.

Think of beta readers as an early detection system for authorly misconceptions about your book's audience, genre, ability to hit tropes or otherwise provide reader satisfaction. Beta readers can help you improve your craft and give you key insights to guide your marketing.

You need deep information about characters, content, or settings outside your personal experience.

Sensitivity readers can help deepen characterization and authenticity for cultural hot topics, historic or geographic details, and language—especially dialogue—that doesn't come out of the author's direct personal experience. Sensitivity readers are often paid subject-matter experts.

"The role that readers play in shaping children's books has become a flash point in a fractious debate about diversity, cultural appropriation, and representation," Alexandra Alter wrote in *The New York Times*, "with some arguing that the reliance on sensitivity readers amounts to censorship."

Others consider it part of the writing process. In the 2022 Festival of Faith & Writing, award-winning children's and YA author Nikki Grimes talked about how she does additional work "to always make sure my storytelling is authentic on every single level."

You want your book to stand on its own.

Beta readers who are unfamiliar with your books or series can tell you if your book really can be read as a stand-alone or out of order and still be a satisfying experience.

You have time to dig more deeply into your project.

Beta readers add time to your production schedule. For example, Hidden Gems' beta reader service has a default of ten days for feedback. Rush services are available for an extra fee. The Spun Yarn service allows their readers three weeks to read and another week for them to collate the feedback for the author. Unpaid beta readers may take longer to get back to you.

Once you have the feedback, you will need additional time for revisions or possibly more beta readers. On the Fully Booked podcast, Yeomans and author Lisa M. Lilly shared several tips about using beta readers, including an approach that uses multiple rounds of beta readers.

If your publishing timeline is tight, consider a professional developmental

editor. Compare costs closely. Beta reader services can be expensive too. Weigh the convenience of a quicker turnaround and the possibility of speedier revisions against the value of multiple opinions.

WHEN MIGHT ARC READERS FIT INTO YOUR PUBLISHING STRATEGY?

Your book is aimed at audiences who value editorial reviews.

If your target audience includes librarians, teachers, booksellers, or other readers whose book purchases are influenced by editorial reviews, it may be worth delaying your publication to pursue ARC readers. Early reviews may help the right readers find your book. A selling quote from a great review is always useful for promotion or advertising.

You have allowed extra time before publication.

ARC readers also add time to your publishing schedule. Many editorial reviewers want the completed manuscript three to six months before publication. Your email subscribers or social media followers may review closer to publication, or you may offer review copies to readers to increase the number of reviews on a previously published book and/or in a particular retailer.

You want numerous reviews.

Can you ever have too many reviews? In contrast to beta readers, you want many ARC readers. Since ARC readers report publicly on their reading experience, they don't create more work for you. You only need to revise if you are planning a second edition.

For more about ARC readers and how to manage the ARC process, see "Your Biggest ARC Team Questions, Answered" in this issue. ■

Laurel Decher

RESOURCES

Strategies for Beta Readers

Fully Booked podcast, episode 9: "Yes, you need Beta Readers. Here's why …" for insights into why and how to use beta readers. https://hiddengemsbooks.com/podcast/episode-9

"Are Beta Readers Worth the Trouble?" by Randy Overbeck for a description of one way to use beta readers. https://readerviews.com/are-beta-readers-worth-the-trouble

"How to Work With Beta Readers" https://writingcooperative.com/how-to-work-with-beta-readers-8200936be30d (See also "Ten Tips for Beta Readers" earlier in this month's issue.)

The Smashwords Marketing Guide (free downloadable ebook [EPUB, MOBI, PDF])—see the "Deep Dive" section for a different take on how to work with beta readers. https://smashwords.com/books/view/305

"Writing Feedback: The Ultimate Guide to Working with Beta Readers" https://thewritelife.com/ultimate-guide-to-beta-readers

"The Difference Between Critique Partners and Beta Readers" from Janice Hardy's Fiction University http://blog.janicehardy.com/2019/01/the-difference-between-critique.html

"How I Became a Sensitivity Reader" https://hiddengemsbooks.com/how-became-sensitivity-reader

"In an Era of Online Outrage, Do Sensitivity Readers Result in Better Books, or Censorship?" by Alexandra Alter https://nytimes.com/2017/12/24/books/in-an-era-of-online-outrage-do-sensitivity-readers-result-in-better-books-or-censorship.html

Where to Find Beta Readers

"The Five Best Ways to Find Beta Readers" https://betabooks.co/blog/post/the-five-best-ways-to-find-beta-readers

Hidden Gems beta reader service. Visit the Author FAQ page on the service's website for a price calculator—found under "How much does it cost?"—and for a list of sample questions to ask your beta readers. https://hiddengemsbooks.com/beta-program-faq

"41 Places to Find a Critique Partner Who Will Help You Improve Your Writing" by Cathy Yardley https://thewritelife.com/find-a-critique-partner

The Spun Yarn beta reader service https://thespunyarn.com/getfeedback

"What are Beta Readers—and How to Find Them" https://blog.reedsy.com/beta-readers

Where to Find ARC Readers

Booksprout (paid service) https://booksprout.co/pricing

Book Sirens (Free if you bring your own ARC readers, or use their paid option.) https://booksirens.com

StoryOrigin (paid service) https://storyoriginapp.com/pricing

Voracious Readers Only (This is a paid service, but their website is being renovated. Sign up to be notified when their service reopens.) https://voraciousreadersonly.com/authors

NetGalley (This is a paid service through an author co-op or accessible through BooksGoSocial at https://bgsauthors.com/pricing.) According to BooksGoSocial, a median of 13 percent of impressions on NetGalley led to one download, and a median of 7 percent of downloads led to a review. https://victoryediting.com/services/netgalley-co-op

Edelweiss (This is a paid service, and a discount is available with an IBPA membership.) https://ibpa-online.org/page/edelweiss-above-the-treeline

Your Biggest ARC Team Questions, Answered

An ARC (Advance Reader or Review Copy) team is a valuable tool in an indie author's arsenal. An engaged ARC team can help you build momentum with solid reviews on launch as well as help with marketing. If your early readers like your book, they might also post about it on social media. Free word of mouth from Bookstagrammers and BookTokers is priceless, especially on or around launch day.

If you don't yet have an ARC team, you can put out an open call in your newsletter or on social media—TikTok, Instagram, and dedicated Facebook groups can work especially well. You could also use services such as BookSprout, BookSirens, or StoryOrigin to find ARC readers.

But how do you handle an ARC team once you have one? What's the best way to manage your team and keep them happy and engaged?

WHAT TO KEEP IN MIND

Communication is key. Communicate with your ARC team often and keep them engaged. Don't just contact your team when you need something. This is a partnership, not a one-way transaction.

You can include language like "ARC Email" in your subject line when sending an update. The reason for this is twofold. First, you're letting them know that they're special, and second, they're more likely to open and read an email related to ARCs. Win-win!

That said, if you want to take it a step further, you could consider individualized communications with the members of your ARC team. Depending on the size of your team, this may be time-consuming, but readers will appreciate the personal touch. You can check in with them, ask what they're reading, or offer updates from your own life. Communicating with members of your ARC team individually will also help keep them accountable, and they will therefore be more likely to post a review.

You can also send your ARC team opportunities to read and review advanced copies for other authors—bonus points if the books are in your subgenre. This is especially effective when you have a large gap between releases. This strategy can be really successful: You're feeding your ARC team with exclusive content and providing value, which your team members are sure to appreciate. Furthermore, it can massively help with lining up your titles in the also-bought section on distribution sites if your team members go on to buy other books by that author.

You could also create a separate ARC and Street Team group or chat thread on Facebook or Discord. Your readers can then talk to each other and generate more buzz—even among themselves—as they discuss your latest plot twist. Additionally, you're granting them something that readers find invaluable: exclusive access to you, the author. Once you create this kind of space for your team members, you could also ask them questions, create polls, and make them feel as if they're part of the process. You could ask them to post links to their reviews or encourage them to create aesthetically pleasing bookish photos for Instagram or Facebook or short videos for TikTok or Instagram Reels. The more they contribute, the more invested they will be in reading your book and seeing it succeed.

AUTHOR, BEWARE

Authors should be aware of several pitfalls when it comes to ARC teams.

Family and friends should not be on your ARC team. Distribution sites, such as Amazon, have been known to remove reviews they identified as left by an author's close friends or relatives. After all, books are a product, and Amazon wants their product reviews to be unbiased, not skewed by friendly reviews.

Do not pay for reviews or offer any sort of incentives in exchange for a review. You need to be clear in your communications with your ARC team that there is no requirement for them to leave a review—it's completely voluntary. They get to read your book, for free, before anyone else. This is their reward. Additionally, they're supporting one of their favorite authors. In a similar vein, ask your team to avoid language such as "in exchange" in their reviews—platforms like Amazon don't like it because it implies that the review wasn't left voluntarily. Any transaction of this sort is against Amazon's—and other retailers'—terms of service.

That said, you could track who leaves reviews in a spreadsheet and simply not offer an ARC for the next book to those who didn't review. This is your prerogative, although it does require a lot of extra administrative legwork. So how do you keep track of your ARC team and who's reviewed what?

TRACKING ARCS AND REVIEWS

When a reader signs up to receive an ARC, they likely have good intentions. They're probably genuinely interested and excited to read your book. However, life does happen, so realistically, you can't expect 100 percent of your ARC team to leave reviews.

If, however, you're sending out hundreds of ARCs and only getting a handful of reviews, it might be a sign that your ARC team consists mainly of freebie seekers who want the free book but who won't leave a review.

To remedy this, you can create a spreadsheet using a program such as Excel, Google Sheets, or Numbers, where you can track information and a number of variables about your ARC team:

- name
- email
- links to social media (Amazon reviewer profile, Goodreads, their book blog, Instagram, TikTok, Twitter, BookBub reader

profile, etc.)

- date you last communicated
- whether you sent an ARC
- whether they published their review
- a copy of their review
- any other information, e.g., which of your books they have read, their reading preferences, or their favorite method of communication (email, Facebook Messenger, text message)

This is, of course, time-consuming, but it may help you weed out the people who consistently request ARC copies but never leave reviews. Only you can decide whether this kind of tracking is worth the time for your author business.

HOW MANY ARC TEAM MEMBERS SHOULD I HAVE?

This is a very individual question and depends on your author business and your goals. Some authors have as little as five or ten ARC readers and rely on organic reviews on launch day. Others have a specific amount and cap the number of ARC team members. This has the benefit of exclusivity and will encourage members to leave reviews for the chance to stay on your team. Some authors don't have an ARC team at all, while others have hundreds or even thousands of members. One Paranormal Romance author sent out over six thousand ARCs of her latest release in April 2022, according to a post in the 20BooksTo50K® Facebook group. The sky is the limit. It's really up to you to decide if you want to manage an ARC Team at all and, if so, how many members you should have.

DECIDE WHAT IS BEST FOR YOU AND YOUR AUTHOR BUSINESS

Managing an ARC team successfully is a lot of work and takes away from the time that you could spend on other tasks, such as writing the next book in your series. If you can afford it, a personal assistant could do this for you. If you can't, then you'll have to weigh the pros and cons yourself. Are the potential rewards associated with successfully running an ARC team worth the time and energy required to run it? If you're seeing little return on your investment, then you may wish to reconsider. You can simply ask for

reviews in the back matter of your books. Plenty of heavy-hitter authors don't have ARC teams and still see a lot of success. But if you can incorporate the management of your team into your day-to-day author activities and see true benefits, then go for it! You're the only one who can figure out and decide what works best for you and your author business.

For more information on how to curate a team of ARC readers, see "Authenticity and Buzz: A Closer Look at What Beta Readers and ARC Readers Have to Offer" in this issue. ■

Kasia Lasinska

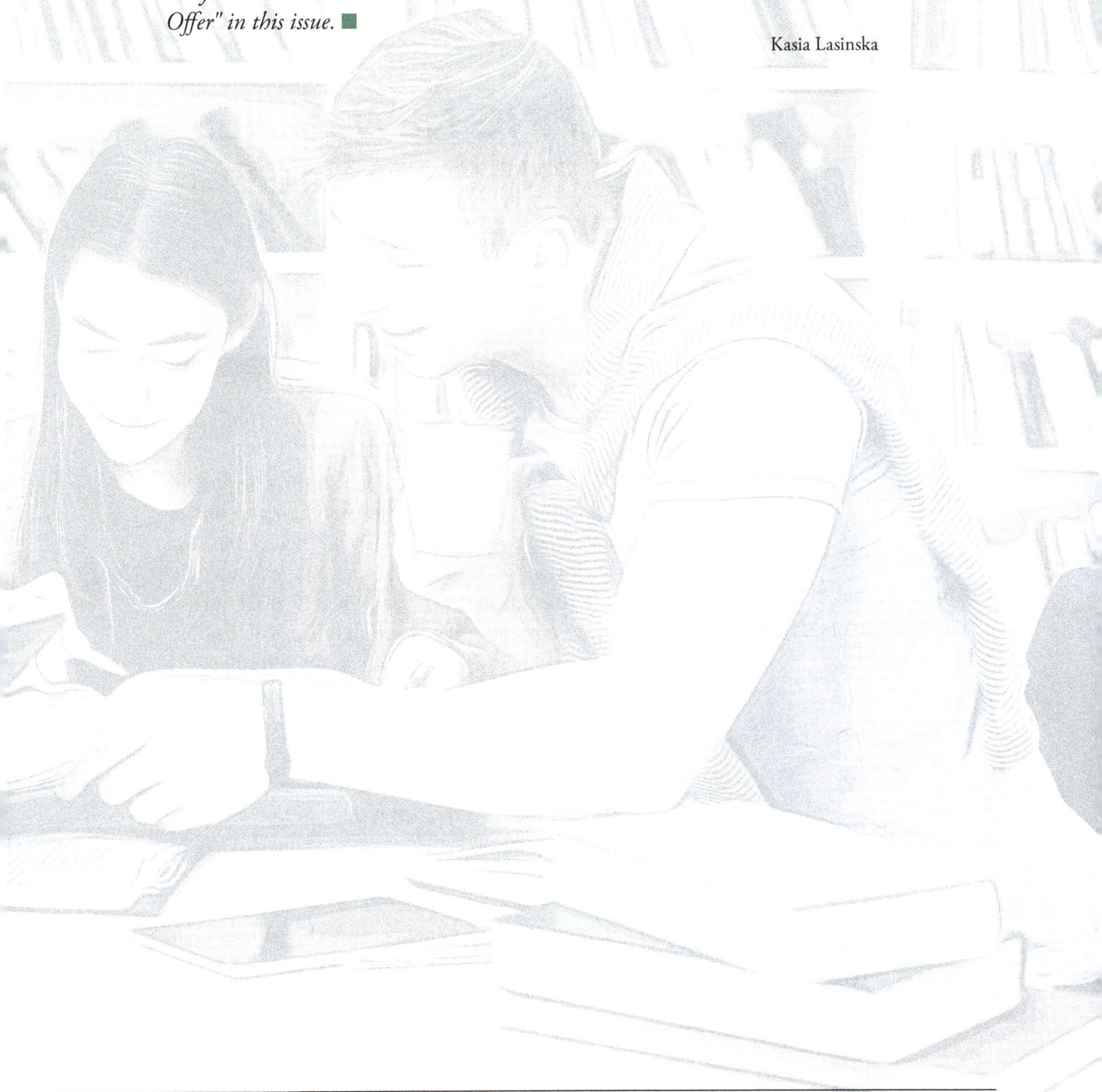

StoryOrigin

HELPING NEW INDIES LEARN TO MANAGE NEWSLETTER MARKETING

Released: 2018

Operating System: Online at https://storyoriginapp.com/

Price:
- Basic: Free (Limited access)
- Standard: $10/month or $100/year (Full access)

Guided Setup is available for a fee

StoryOrigin is, by all measures, a wealth of resources for an author first starting out or trying to organize and build their publishing business.

This online web app boasts three major functions: building your mailing list, finding reviewers, and promoting your offerings. At this point, you may think, "Well, I already have BookFunnel for that," and if that's your only consideration, you would be right.

What makes StoryOrigin shine is not only its tech but also the full wealth of knowledge it provides that will guide you to using this site to its full potential.

Let's take a deeper look at StoryOrigin, its features and benefits, and the articles that are best for a quick start and more in-depth information.

KNOW THE LINGO

Before you get started, you'll want to know some of the industry terms StoryOrigin uses in its program. If you're an indie author veteran, everything should seem old hat, but if you're new to the publishing world, here are some of the more common terms you might run into:

Promotions/Promos: a general term for using someone else's platform to tell the story of your book. Promos come in various forms, but we will focus on:

- **Group Promos:** A group of authors team up and make a single offering (giveaway, bundle, etc.) to all their audiences.
- **Newsletter Swaps:** An author trades a mention in their newsletter for a mention in another author's.

Landing Pages: This is a standalone web page where a visitor "lands" after they click on a link in an email or an ad.

Reader Magnet: This is an offering, usually a short story or the first book in a series, made to readers in exchange for joining their mailing list.

Universal Book Link/Universal Audio Link: This is a short link to a web page with links to all the stores where the ebook or audiobook is available. The store they choose traditionally becomes the default.

Beta Copy: This is a book sent out to a reading team (known as "beta readers") to detect any issues before the final edit.

Review Copy: This is a copy of the finished book sent to readers in hopes of a review.

OPENING AN ACCOUNT

Opening an account in StoryOrigin is quite straightforward. It'll ask you for your email address and to create a password that will be confirmed through your email provider.

Once confirmed, you can log on to access the page that asks you to sign up for the Standard Plan. We'll return to that in a moment, but for now, click your email address in the upper right-hand corner (marked with the green arrow).

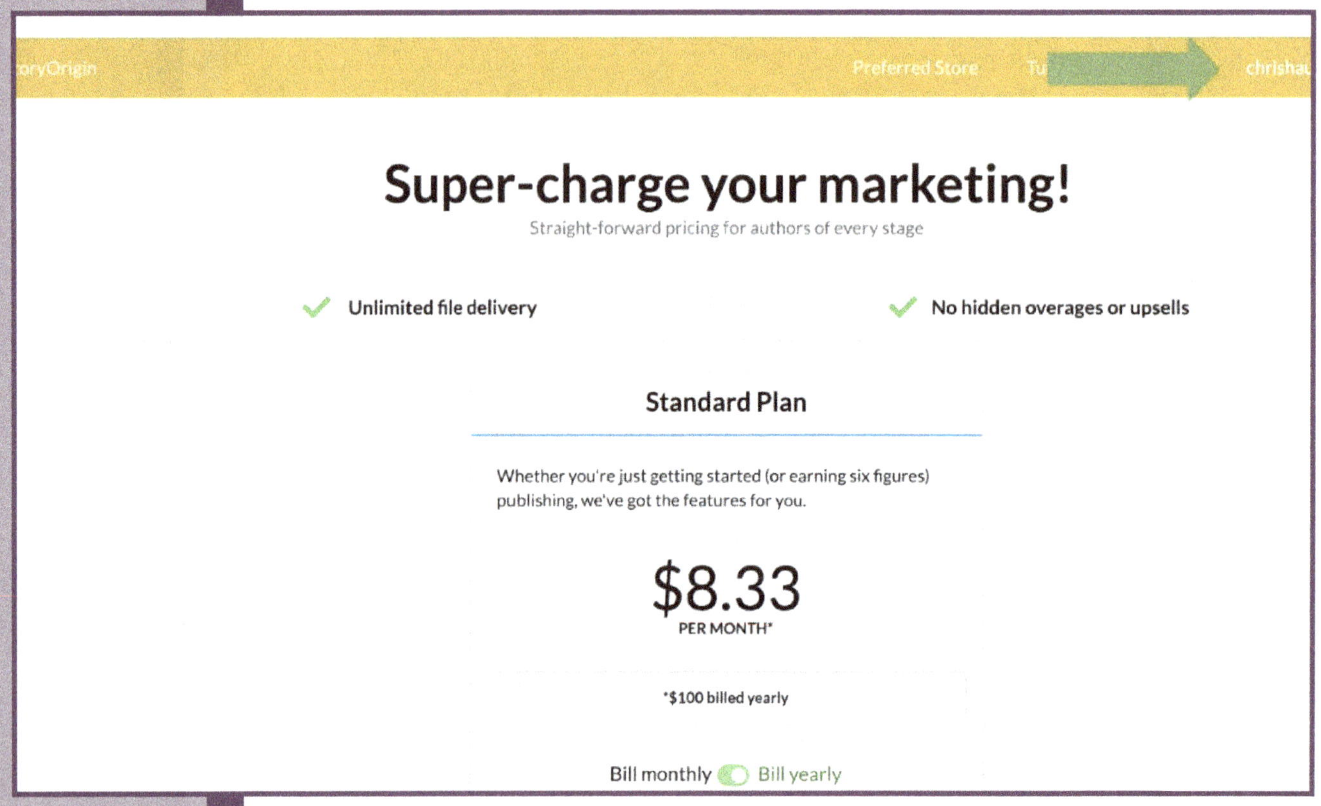

Preferred Store
Super-charge your marketing!
Straight-forward pricing for authors of every stage
Unlimited file delivery
No hidden overages or upsells
Standard Plan
Whether you're just getting started (or earning six figures) publishing, we've got the features for you.
$8.33
PER MONTH*
*$100 billed yearly
Bill monthly
Bill yearly

That will produce a drop-down box with several options. We're going to start with the Author Dashboard, the brains of StoryOrigin.

chrishaun@allazar.com
Reviewer Dashboard
Author Dashboard
Account
Logout

With the free Basic Tier, you see a large banner telling you that you have the basic plan, which allows you to set up file delivery and use the goal tracker. Even so, it's simple to take a look at what benefits you would get for your ten dollars a month with the Standard Plan.

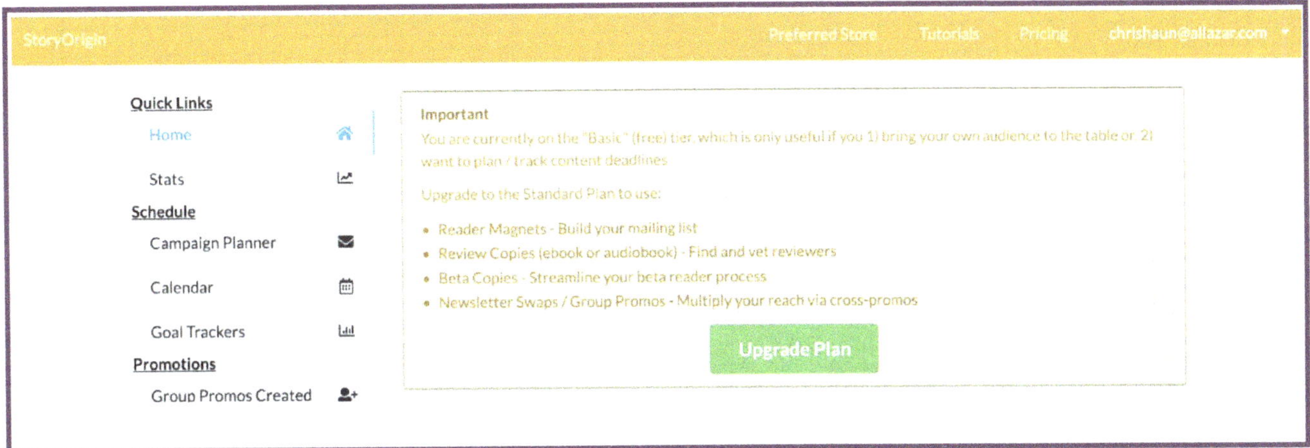

A QUICK LOOK UNDER THE HOOD

Data controls the world around us. Being able to weigh your options and measure your results makes all the difference in this business. StoryOrigin will tell you the open rates on any prospective list you may want to swap with on the site, as well as create tracking links for swaps and campaigns so you can see how many folks clicked your link.

Let's take a look.

At the menu on the left, under "Schedule," click "Campaign Planner."

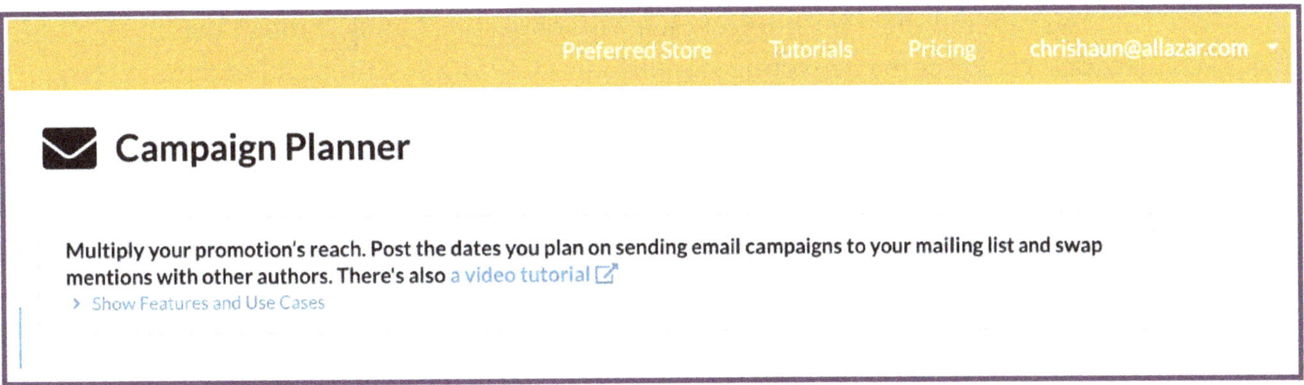

It will take you to a page that lists your future campaigns. Under the heading, you will see this box that describes what the Campaign Planner is, a video tutorial, and cases where you can see how this feature is used. This video tutorial walks you through planning a campaign step-by-step. Below that is a dropdown menu labeled "Show Features and Use Cases."

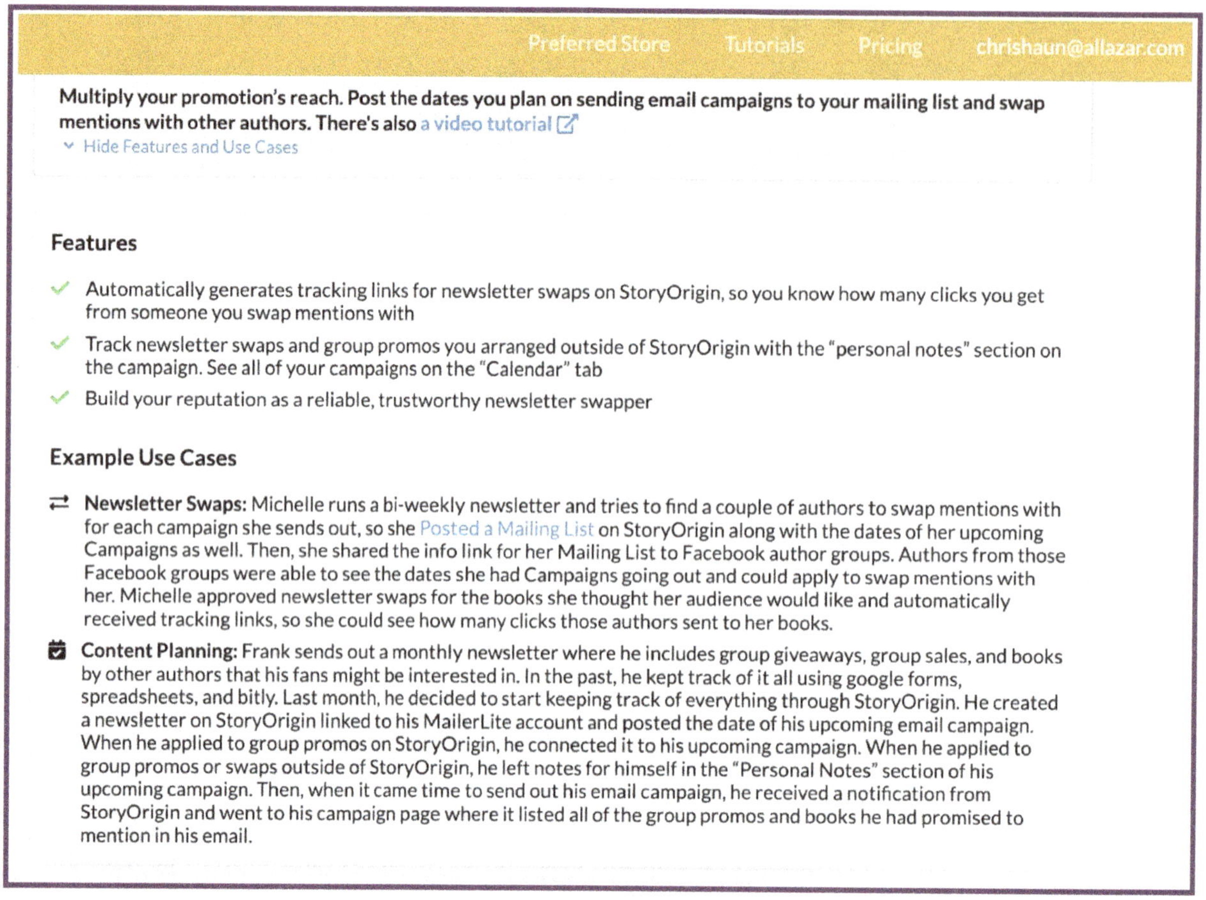

Preferred Store Tutorials Pricing chrishaun@allazar.com

Multiply your promotion's reach. Post the dates you plan on sending email campaigns to your mailing list and swap mentions with other authors. There's also a video tutorial

Hide Features and Use Cases

Features

- Automatically generates tracking links for newsletter swaps on StoryOrigin, so you know how many clicks you get from someone you swap mentions with
- Track newsletter swaps and group promos you arranged outside of StoryOrigin with the "personal notes" section on the campaign. See all of your campaigns on the "Calendar" tab
- Build your reputation as a reliable, trustworthy newsletter swapper

Example Use Cases

Newsletter Swaps: Michelle runs a bi-weekly newsletter and tries to find a couple of authors to swap mentions with for each campaign she sends out, so she Posted a Mailing List on StoryOrigin along with the dates of her upcoming Campaigns as well. Then, she shared the info link for her Mailing List to Facebook author groups. Authors from those Facebook groups were able to see the dates she had Campaigns going out and could apply to swap mentions with her. Michelle approved newsletter swaps for the books she thought her audience would like and automatically received tracking links, so she could see how many clicks those authors sent to her books.

Content Planning: Frank sends out a monthly newsletter where he includes group giveaways, group sales, and books by other authors that his fans might be interested in. In the past, he kept track of it all using google forms, spreadsheets, and bitly. Last month, he decided to start keeping track of everything through StoryOrigin. He created a newsletter on StoryOrigin linked to his MailerLite account and posted the date of his upcoming email campaign. When he applied to group promos on StoryOrigin, he connected it to his upcoming campaign. When he applied to group promos or swaps outside of StoryOrigin, he left notes for himself in the "Personal Notes" section of his upcoming campaign. Then, when it came time to send out his email campaign, he received a notification from StoryOrigin and went to his campaign page where it listed all of the group promos and books he had promised to mention in his email.

StoryOrigin not only shows you how to use a tool but also gives you the scenarios that work best for that tool as well as links to other pertinent steps and their instructions. (Note: Since some of the tools perform very similar functions, you will see the same message at times. But this is a brief overview—the Get Started Guide has all the information you need.)

You will find these at the top of each page of the site. Going through these articles will lower the marketing learning curve, saving you time and money.

Using the features is simple and straightforward. Follow the same steps.

To use the Newsletter Swap/Promo features:

1. Under the "Get involved in the community" heading, you can choose either "Browse Newsletter Swaps" or "Browse Group Promos." For these examples, I'll be using the "Browse Newsletter Swap."

Get involved in the community

Browse Newsletter Swaps | Browse Group Promos

1) Build mailing list 2) Find reviewers 3) Increase sales

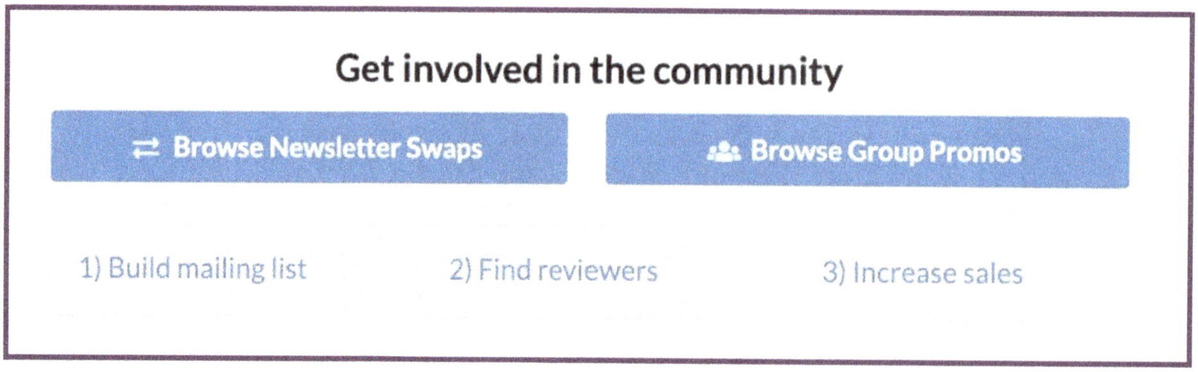

2. That will take you to this next page where you will see several offerings and a filter. The filter itself includes a variety of customization options:

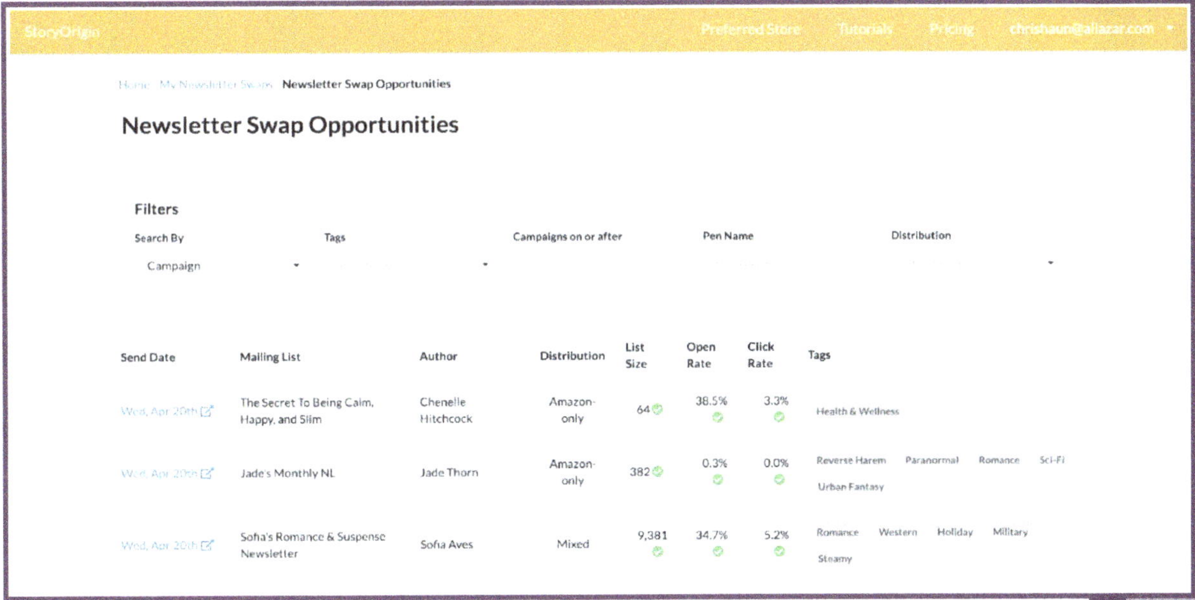

Newsletter Swap Opportunities
Newsletter Swap Opportunities
Filters
Search By
Tags
Campaigns on or after
Pen Name
Distribution
Campaign
Send Date
Mailing List
Author
Distribution
List Size
Open Rate
Click Rate
Tags
The Secret To Being Calm, Happy, and Slim
Chenelle Hitchcock
Amazon-only
64
38.5%
3.3%
Health & Wellness
Jade's Monthly NL
Jade Thorn
Amazon-only
382
0.3%
0.0%
Reverse Harem
Paranormal
Romance
Sci-Fi
Urban Fantasy
Sofia's Romance & Suspense Newsletter
Sofia Aves
Mixed
9,381
34.7%
5.2%
Romance
Western
Holiday
Military
Steamy

a. The "Search By" option allows you to choose from several categories, including:

i. Campaign: a planned group of promos and swaps that run over a certain period of time

ii. Newsletter Swap: one-time reciprocated slots in a newsletter in which you pick a time on the other author's newsletter and they choose a slot on yours

iii. Mailing list: allows you to choose a specific mailing list

b. "Tags" allow you to choose the genre you want to swap in.

c. "Campaigns on or after" allows you to find campaigns within a certain time frame.

d. "Pen Name" allows you to search by name.

e. "Distribution" allows you to choose if you want Amazon-only distribution, wide distribution, or both options.

3. Once you've entered your parameters, a list of potential swaps appears. Click the entry that interests you and look over the requirements. Once you've found one you like, click on the link.

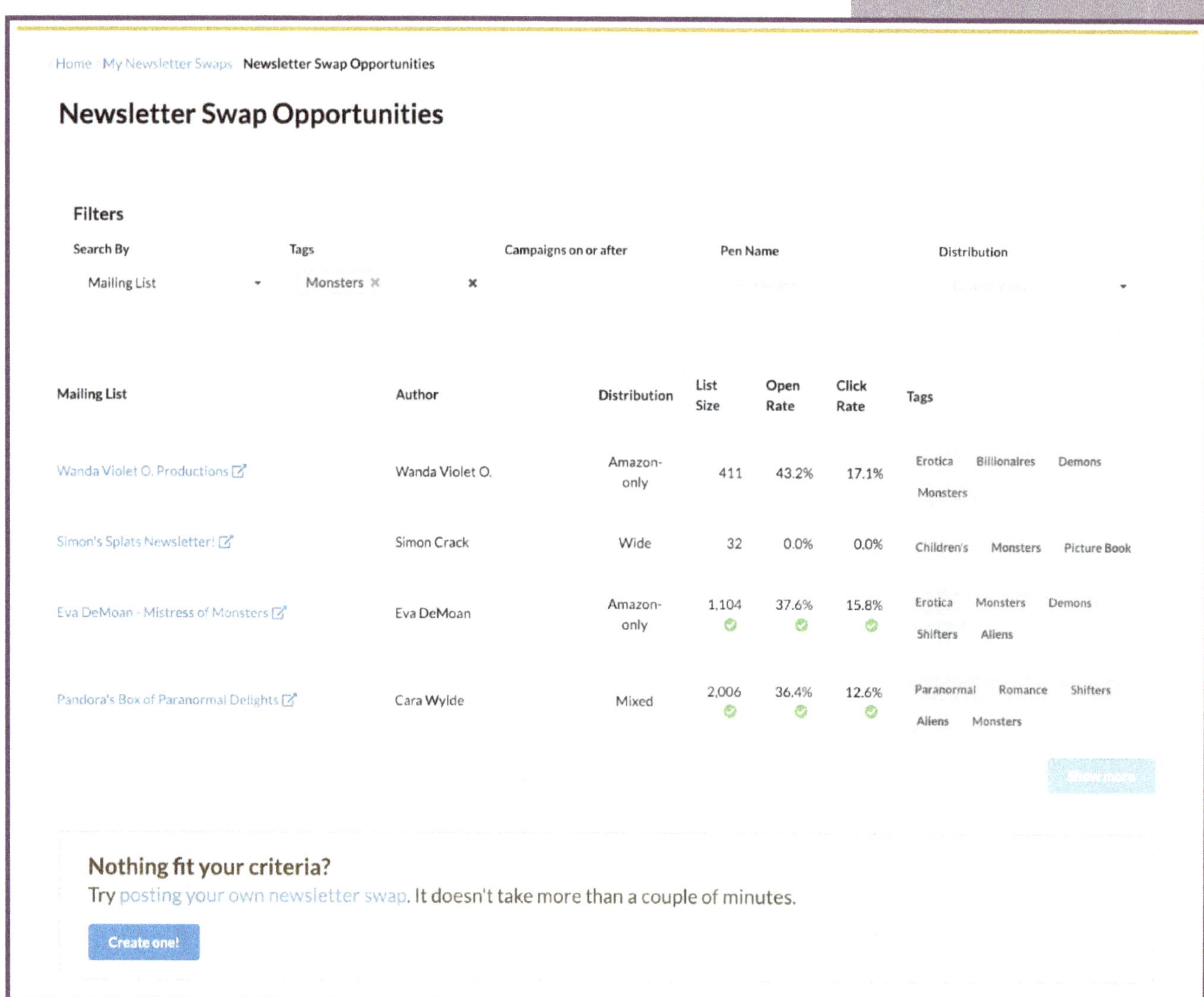

Home / My Newsletter Swaps / Newsletter Swap Opportunities

Newsletter Swap Opportunities

Filters

Search By	Tags	Campaigns on or after	Pen Name	Distribution
Mailing List	Monsters			

Mailing List	Author	Distribution	List Size	Open Rate	Click Rate	Tags
Wanda Violet O. Productions	Wanda Violet O.	Amazon-only	411	43.2%	17.1%	Erotica, Billionaires, Demons, Monsters
Simon's Splats Newsletter!	Simon Crack	Wide	32	0.0%	0.0%	Children's, Monsters, Picture Book
Eva DeMoan - Mistress of Monsters	Eva DeMoan	Amazon-only	1,104	37.6%	15.8%	Erotica, Monsters, Demons, Shifters, Aliens
Pandora's Box of Paranormal Delights	Cara Wylde	Mixed	2,006	36.4%	12.6%	Paranormal, Romance, Shifters, Aliens, Monsters

Nothing fit your criteria?

Try posting your own newsletter swap. It doesn't take more than a couple of minutes.

Create one!

4. The next page will give you the number of subscribers and their open and click rates.

   If you click "Past Campaigns," you will get a list of how the newsletter performed in other swaps, giving you added insight that lets you make informed decisions.

5. Click on the green "Apply to Swap" button, and the next page has the books available for swaps and other details about the newsletter. You can also look at the books available for swap. Books that have the Universal Book Link will be listed with either a shopping cart (the sales link) or a reader magnet.

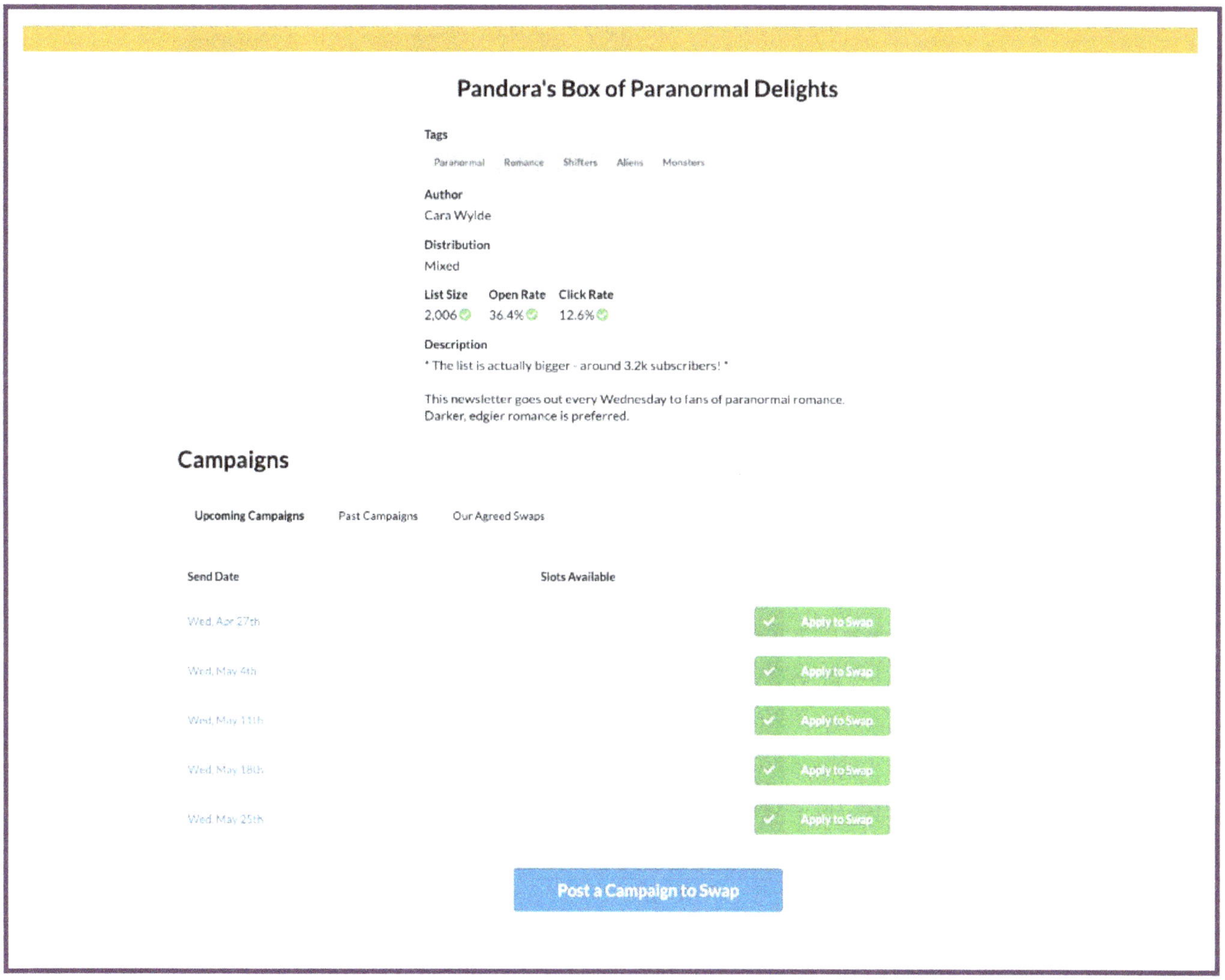

Pandora's Box of Paranormal Delights

Tags
Paranormal Romance Shifters Aliens Monsters

Author
Cara Wylde

Distribution
Mixed

List Size	Open Rate	Click Rate
2,006	36.4%	12.6%

Description
* The list is actually bigger - around 3.2k subscribers! *

This newsletter goes out every Wednesday to fans of paranormal romance.
Darker, edgier romance is preferred.

Campaigns

Upcoming Campaigns Past Campaigns Our Agreed Swaps

Send Date	Slots Available	
Wed, Apr 27th		Apply to Swap
Wed, May 4th		Apply to Swap
Wed, May 11th		Apply to Swap
Wed, May 18th		Apply to Swap
Wed, May 25th		Apply to Swap

Post a Campaign to Swap

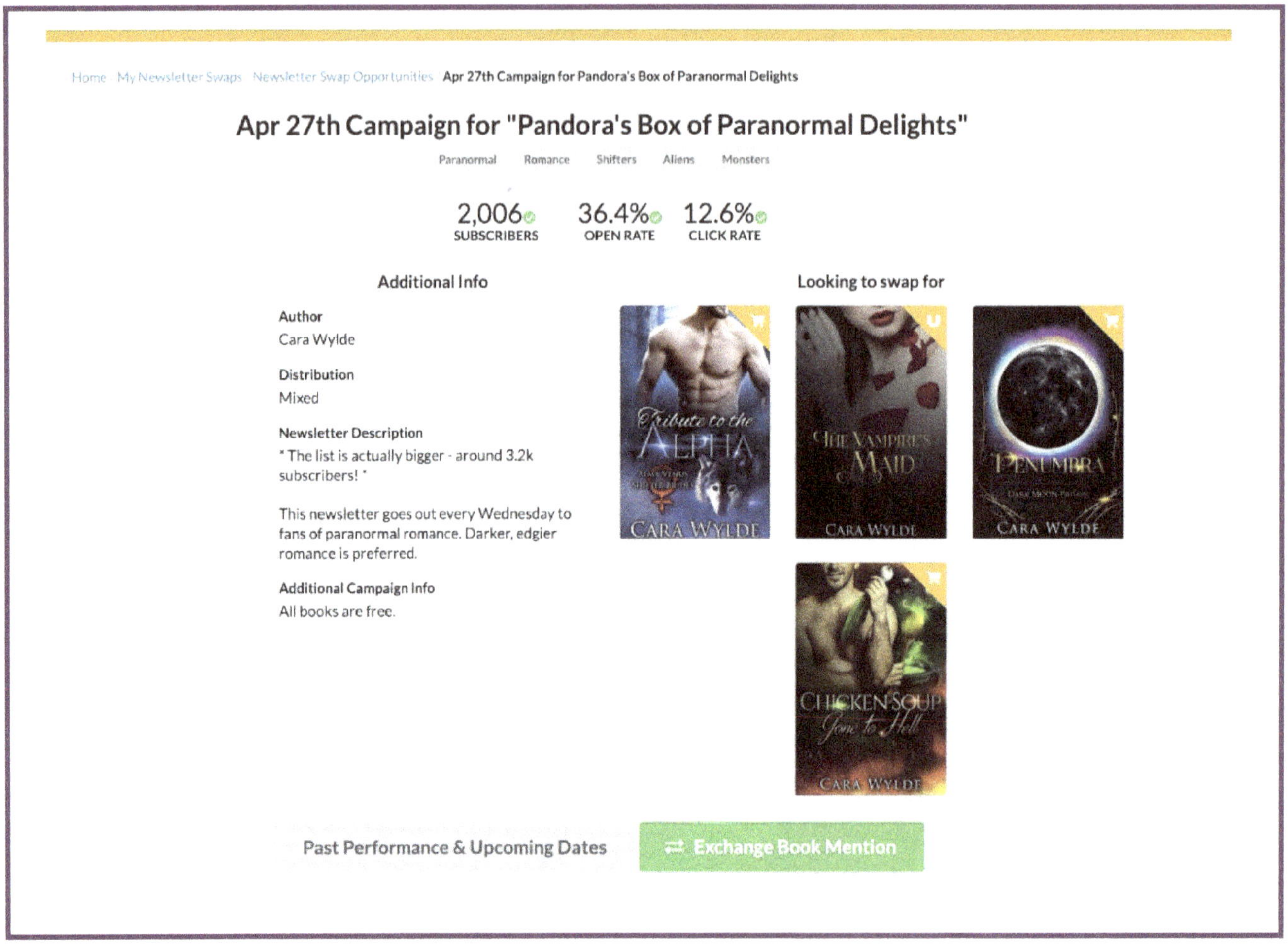

Home · My Newsletter Swaps · Newsletter Swap Opportunities · Apr 27th Campaign for Pandora's Box of Paranormal Delights

Apr 27th Campaign for "Pandora's Box of Paranormal Delights"

Paranormal · Romance · Shifters · Aliens · Monsters

2,006 SUBSCRIBERS · 36.4% OPEN RATE · 12.6% CLICK RATE

Additional Info

Author
Cara Wylde

Distribution
Mixed

Newsletter Description
* The list is actually bigger - around 3.2k subscribers! *

This newsletter goes out every Wednesday to fans of paranormal romance. Darker, edgier romance is preferred.

Additional Campaign Info
All books are free.

Looking to swap for

Tribute to the Alpha — Cara Wylde

The Vampire's Maid — Cara Wylde

Penumbra — Cara Wylde

Chicken Soup Gone to Hell — Cara Wylde

Past Performance & Upcoming Dates

Exchange Book Mention

A WEALTH OF INFORMATION

The indie industry is built primarily of tribal knowledge, skills that authors develop through doing the work or asking people in their circles. So at times, all these tools might confuse a new author.

In this section, StoryOrigin has gathered and arranged the knowledge you need to use these powerful tools effectively through tutorials and author case studies.

At the top of the page, click on "Tutorials."

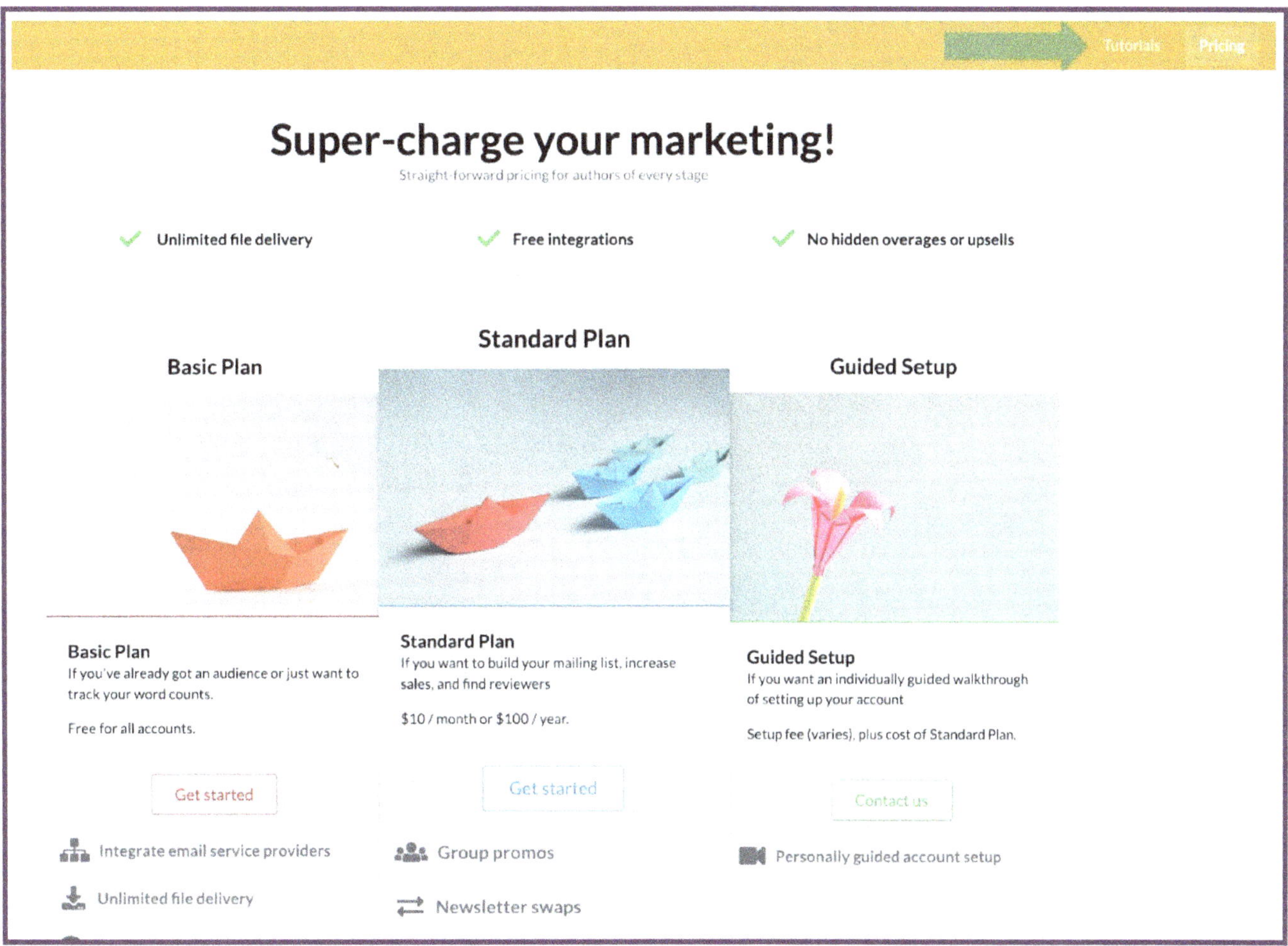

If you forgot where you saw that one article or that one feature you need, all the StoryOrigin text, video, and quick start guides are listed here, giving you a glimpse at the tools before diving in.

Each video showcases a tool and the step-by-step process for using it so you can follow along or refer to it as a reference if you get stuck.

StoryOrigin's combination of data and education was built for an author coming from zero—or nearly so—to the author who wants to make better, more informed, and educated business moves. ■

Chrishaun Keller-Hanna

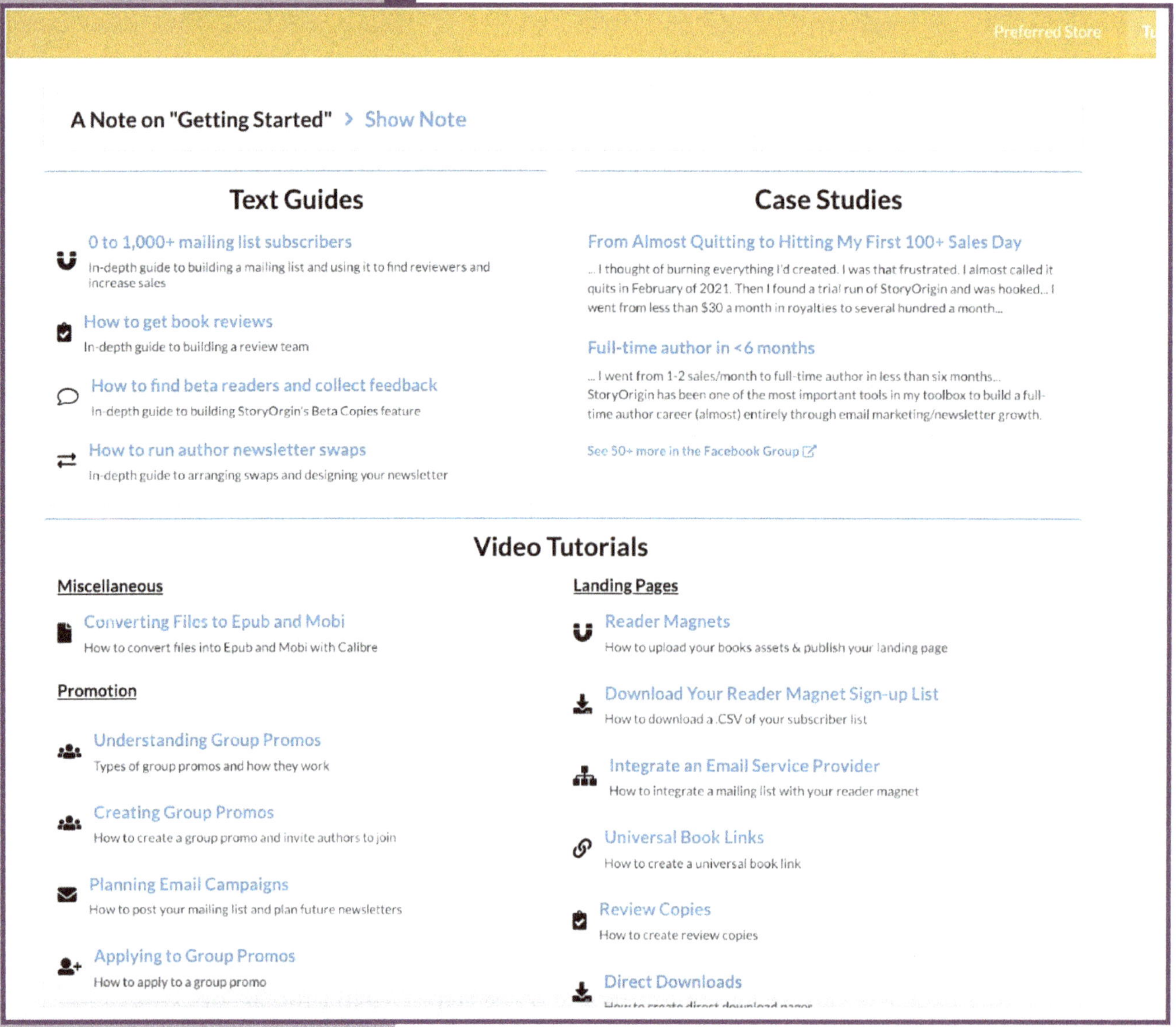

Preferred Store

A Note on "Getting Started" > Show Note

Text Guides

0 to 1,000+ mailing list subscribers
In-depth guide to building a mailing list and using it to find reviewers and increase sales

How to get book reviews
In-depth guide to building a review team

How to find beta readers and collect feedback
In-depth guide to building StoryOrgin's Beta Copies feature

How to run author newsletter swaps
In-depth guide to arranging swaps and designing your newsletter

Case Studies

From Almost Quitting to Hitting My First 100+ Sales Day
... I thought of burning everything I'd created. I was that frustrated. I almost called it quits in February of 2021. Then I found a trial run of StoryOrigin and was hooked... I went from less than $30 a month in royalties to several hundred a month...

Full-time author in <6 months
... I went from 1-2 sales/month to full-time author in less than six months... StoryOrigin has been one of the most important tools in my toolbox to build a full-time author career (almost) entirely through email marketing/newsletter growth.

See 50+ more in the Facebook Group

Video Tutorials

Miscellaneous

Converting Files to Epub and Mobi
How to convert files into Epub and Mobi with Calibre

Promotion

Understanding Group Promos
Types of group promos and how they work

Creating Group Promos
How to create a group promo and invite authors to join

Planning Email Campaigns
How to post your mailing list and plan future newsletters

Applying to Group Promos
How to apply to a group promo

Landing Pages

Reader Magnets
How to upload your books assets & publish your landing page

Download Your Reader Magnet Sign-up List
How to download a .CSV of your subscriber list

Integrate an Email Service Provider
How to integrate a mailing list with your reader magnet

Universal Book Links
How to create a universal book link

Review Copies
How to create review copies

Direct Downloads

Tech Tools

Courtesy of IndieAuthorTools.com
Got a tool you love and want to share with us?
Submit a tool at IndieAuthorTools.com

BetaBooks

Organize and search the feedback from your beta readers with ease with this online app. It enables authors to post a manuscript online, find people to read it, and to collect the feedback. The BetaBooks site is intuitive and easy-to-navigate. There are three program tiers – from free to $34.99 monthly. And you can "turn off" the subscription during the months it is not being used.
https://betabooks.co/

Scribophile

Scribophile is an online writing workshop and community. It bills itself as "the writing group to join if you want to find beta readers, get the best feedback around, learn how to get published…." There's no charge to join, but as part of the community, you are expected to critique the work of other members.
https://www.scribophile.com/

Marlowe

Marlowe is one smart, fiction-savvy bot. Think of her as a combo developmental editor, beta reader, and copy editor. She produces 32-page full-color reports in less than 15 minutes, giving a straightforward critique of your novel to strengthen its pacing, story beats, and writing. Developed by Authors A.I., the artificial intelligence evaluates fiction of more than 20,000 words.
https://authors.ai/

BookSirens

Grow your Advanced Reader Copy (ARC) team with BookSirens. If the online service accepts your manuscript for promotion, you're charged a one-time, nominal listing fee. After that, you pay $2 per reader who downloads your books to read.
https://booksirens.com/

CritiqueMatch

Simplify the process of finding the right critique partner or beta readers with CritiqueMatch's free service. Or if you prefer, you can use the online platform to hire vetted, top-rated freelancers for critique or editing services.
https://www.critiquematch.com

The Reader Magnet Revolution

MODERNIZING THE TRADITIONAL APPROACH TO ATTRACTING AN AUDIENCE

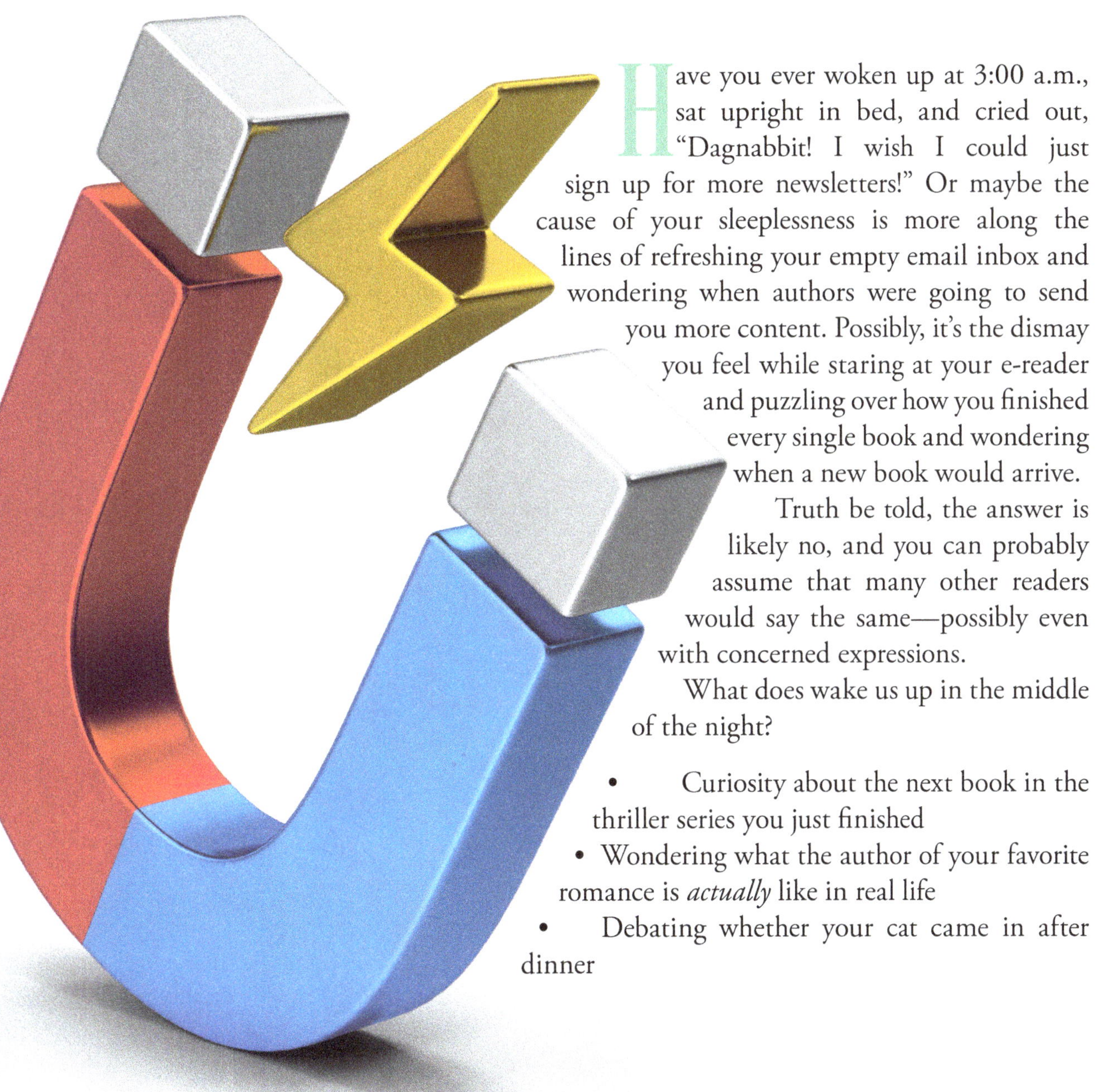

Have you ever woken up at 3:00 a.m., sat upright in bed, and cried out, "Dagnabbit! I wish I could just sign up for more newsletters!" Or maybe the cause of your sleeplessness is more along the lines of refreshing your empty email inbox and wondering when authors were going to send you more content. Possibly, it's the dismay you feel while staring at your e-reader and puzzling over how you finished every single book and wondering when a new book would arrive.

Truth be told, the answer is likely no, and you can probably assume that many other readers would say the same—possibly even with concerned expressions.

What does wake us up in the middle of the night?

- Curiosity about the next book in the thriller series you just finished
- Wondering what the author of your favorite romance is *actually* like in real life
- Debating whether your cat came in after dinner

Or as an author, maybe you wake up with questions like these:

- How can I connect better with my readers?
- How can I be more human to my audience, more than just "that author of those books I like"?
- What might my readers like to hear from me in addition to more books?

TRADITIONAL READER MAGNETS

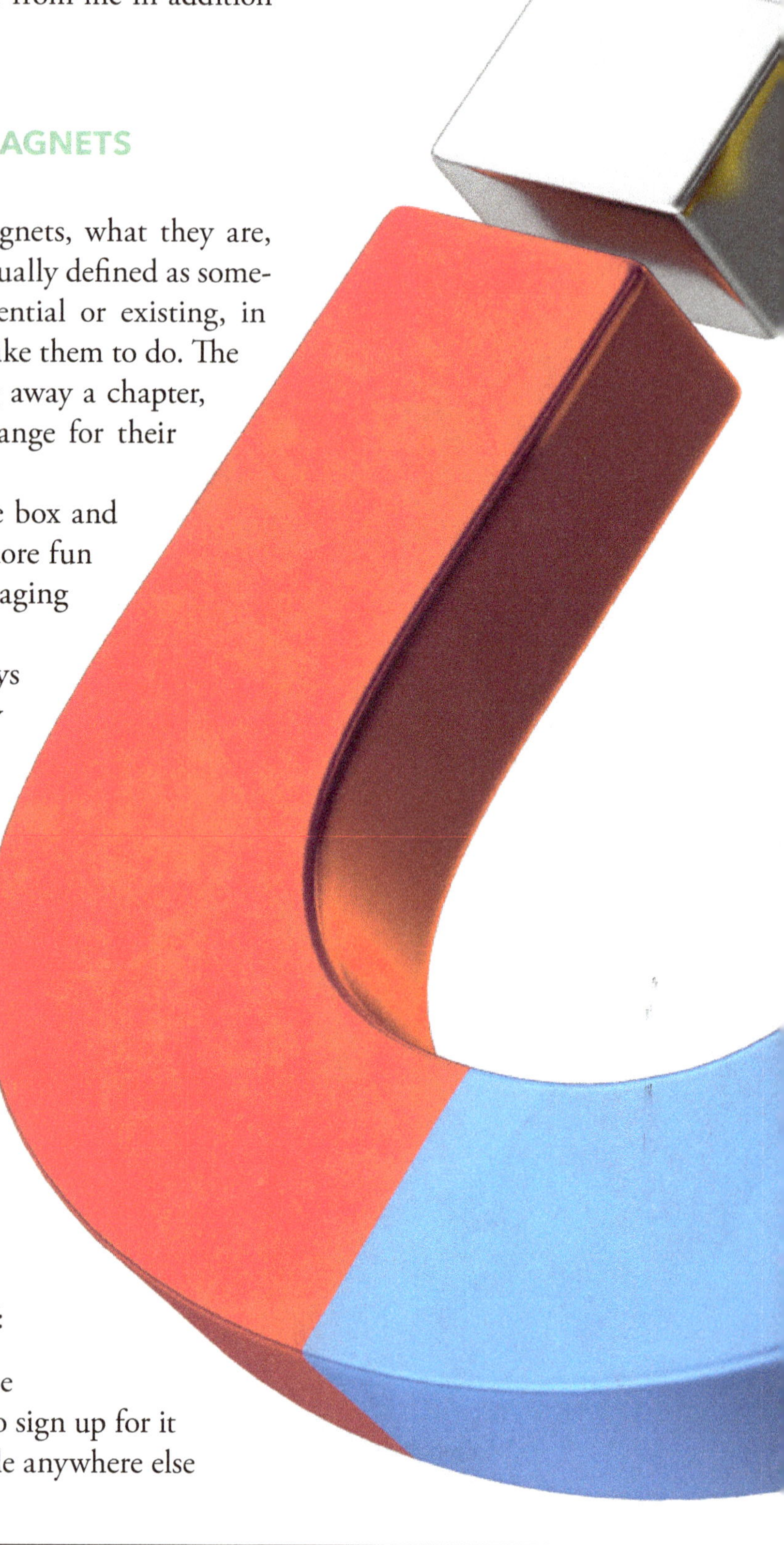

Books have been written about reader magnets, what they are, and how to use them. A reader magnet is usually defined as something you give away to your readers, potential or existing, in exchange for them doing something you'd like them to do. The most common process is the author giving away a chapter, a novella, or even an entire book in exchange for their sign-up to your mailing list.

But let's see if we can crawl outside the box and identify less-traveled paths that might be more fun for you as the author to create and more engaging for your readers to discover.

As authors, you don't know who buys and reads your books until they directly connect with you. They are, as sad as it may sound, just a number. Sure, we could stop there. Authors write books; readers read them. Authors write more; readers read more. It's worked just fine for decades, if not centuries.

So why a reader magnet?

Relationship.

If you can strengthen that author/reader relationship, you possibly gain a longer-term, deeper connection with your readers.

How can we do that?

One tactic is reader magnets.

Usually, the magnet is along the lines of:

- a secret chapter available nowhere else
- a novella only accessible to those who sign up for it
- a complete book, usually not available anywhere else

They click or go to your sign-up page, enter their email address, and you deliver what you promised. After this point, you build that relationship by sending them follow-up emails which, ideally, strengthen that relationship you've now started.

There you have it: the traditional reader-magnet process.

THE NONREADING READER MAGNET

There's absolutely nothing wrong with the traditional method of the reader magnet. In fact, it's a highly recommended author tactic. But what if you tweaked that reader idea just a tad?

There is certainly a strong case for thinking that readers read and want more to read from you, the author. In fact, experts in the industry strongly recommend that you use your wordsmithing talents to attract new readers by … well, by using your wordsmithing talents and offering them more of your writing.

But what if the author offered not words on a page or chapters in a book but something from a different medium?

Have you ever noticed that when you hear someone on a podcast and then you meet them in real life you feel as if you already have a bit of a connection with them? This differs from the connection you have with an author when you read their books.

When someone's voice, quite literally, is in your head, coming through your ears while you're walking in the woods, driving the car, or doing the dishes, you have a different dimension in which to experience that person. It's using a different sense and even using different organs. You hear intonations in their voice, their accent, and maybe even how they say certain words or phrases.

It's just one example of how mediums differ from each other. Other examples of reader magnets use yet more media to relate to your reader. Each one offers a slightly different take on the same topic. Nonreading reader-magnet ideas span a wide range of options. Why not see what triggers your creative senses? Although it's certainly not an exhaustive list, these alternative reader magnets can include:

- a **video** you did on YouTube
- a **playlist** you created on YouTube (Pro tip: Playlists can be made up of your videos or videos from others—think of it like a curated list.)
- a **Spotify playlist** of music, such as music you play in the background when you write or songs you think would be the soundtrack for the film version of your book
- a **blooper reel** of deleted scenes or chapters
- a **character sketch** of a character who got cut from the cast
- **artwork** from your cover
- a **detailed map** of your fantasy world
- an audio recording from your audiobook narrator (e.g. **a free audio chapter**)
- an audio recording from you, the author
- a **behind-the-scenes monologue**
- a **virtual video tour** of your writing space
- an **over-my-shoulder screen recording** of you writing in one of your books (daring!), maybe with your narration as you write
- a **quiz** about a character in your book to test your reader's true connection with your characters
- an **interview** with one of your characters (get a friend to help you or actually switch hats and act as both yourself and the character)
- an **auto-responder series** using your email service provider (something like the YouTube or Spotify playlist but with curated emails with a specific theme, e.g., 10 Days in 10 Emails in the Life of Thaddeus Persmicken)
- a **survey** asking your readers for their feedback or a book- or story-specific survey
- a **mini-course** of either something practical or maybe a How To _____ (e.g., Witchcraft) based on the genre of your book

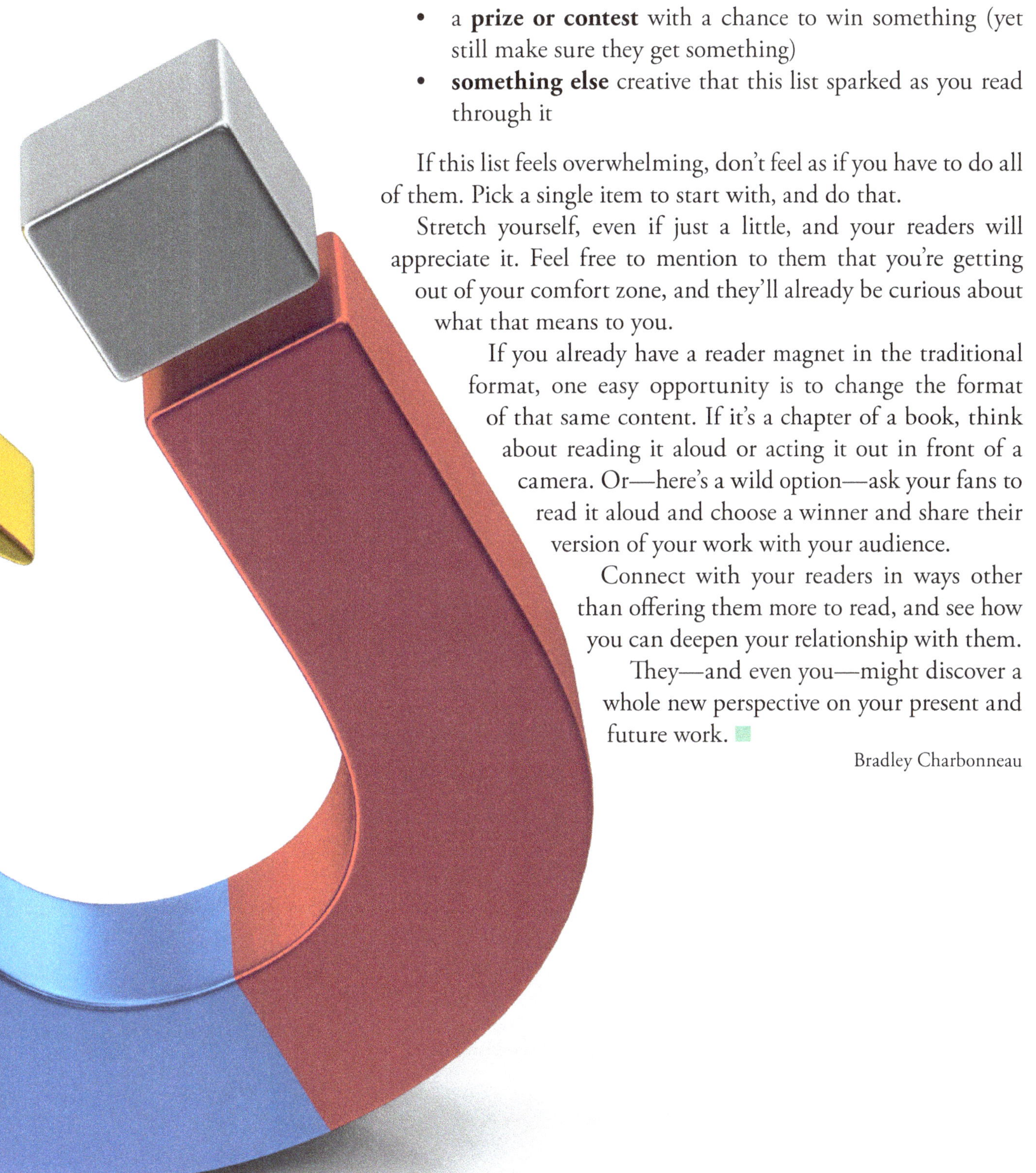

- a **prize or contest** with a chance to win something (yet still make sure they get something)
- **something else** creative that this list sparked as you read through it

If this list feels overwhelming, don't feel as if you have to do all of them. Pick a single item to start with, and do that.

Stretch yourself, even if just a little, and your readers will appreciate it. Feel free to mention to them that you're getting out of your comfort zone, and they'll already be curious about what that means to you.

If you already have a reader magnet in the traditional format, one easy opportunity is to change the format of that same content. If it's a chapter of a book, think about reading it aloud or acting it out in front of a camera. Or—here's a wild option—ask your fans to read it aloud and choose a winner and share their version of your work with your audience.

Connect with your readers in ways other than offering them more to read, and see how you can deepen your relationship with them. They—and even you—might discover a whole new perspective on your present and future work.

Bradley Charbonneau

Podcasts We Love

I Should Be Writing

https://murverse.com/podcasts/isbw/

This award-winning show dispenses advice and encouragement for beginning writers. Catch it live on Twitch at 3 p.m. (Eastern time) Tuesdays and Thursdays or listen to the edited version later in the podcast feed. I Should Be Writing has been hosted by Mur Lafferty since 2005.

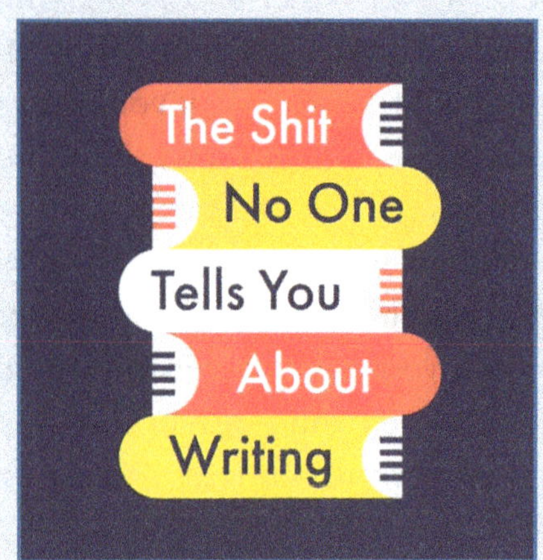

The Shit No One Tells You About Writing

https://podcasts.apple.com/us/podcast/the-shit-no-one-tells-you-about-writing/id1530250126

Want to learn more about the craft and business side of writing and publishing? Listen to The Shit No One Tells You About Writing. Host Bianca Marais interviews authors, agents, editors, and others involved in getting a book to market. Her co-hosts, literary agents Carly Watters and CeCe Lyra, read and critique query letters and opening pages in their Books with Hooks segment.

Author Like a Boss

https://podcasts.apple.com/us/podcast/author-like-a-boss-podcast/id1367276836

Ella Barnard interviews successful authors about their best writing, marketing, and mindset secrets on Author Like a Boss. She says the weekly show is for indie authors "who want to publish stories that readers love, utilize marketing that works, make more money with their writing, and enjoy the process!"

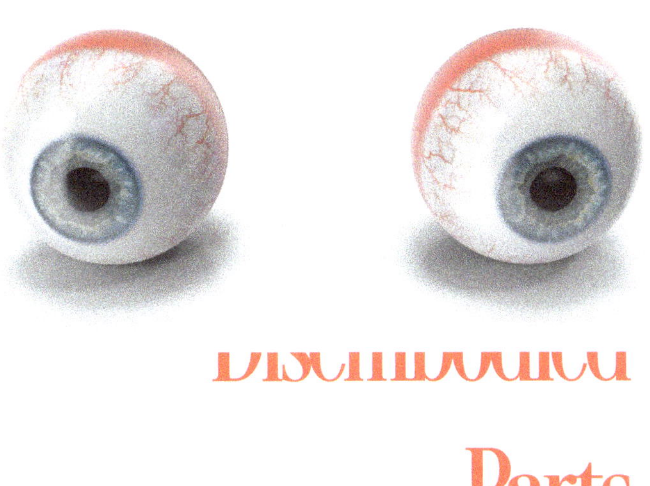

Disembodied Parts

ANCHORING YOUR ANATOMICAL DESCRIPTIONS IN REALITY

"Your eyes touch me physically."
—"The Warrior," performed by Scandal, written by Holly Knight and Nick Gilder

Oh, the amazing wandering body parts. The absolute horror inflicted upon readers as eyes fly, hands inch around, and hearts roam the world. The term "wandering body parts" refers to the sentences in which body parts seem to act on their own accord, as if separate from the person to whom they belong.

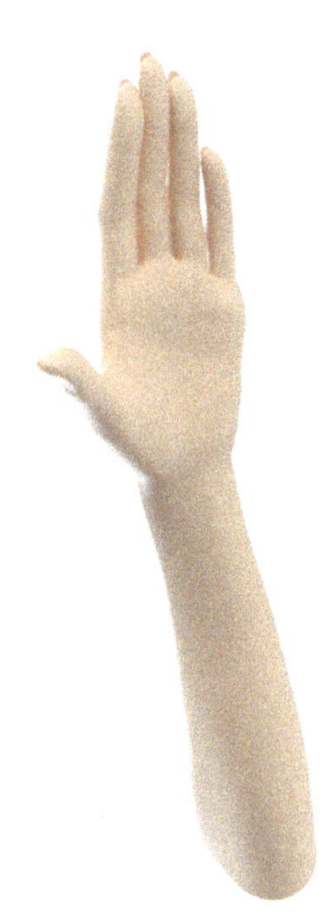

Unless you're writing a horror story, you want those body parts to stay put. Yet writing wandering body parts, also known as floating or autonomous body parts, is such an easy thing to do. It's hard to find a book that doesn't have a body part behaving badly. "When I first started writing, body parts flew all over the place," says author and editor Leila Kirkconnell. "But ever since I learned about them, I end up seeing them everywhere, not only in editing first drafts, but in my daily reading of published books."

In Scandal's 1984 song "The Warrior," the line "Your eyes touch me physically" gives a perfect example of this. It's impossible for eyes to touch someone. Can you imagine how gross that would be if someone's eyeballs popped out of their head and flew over to touch you? But body parts fly all over the place in writing—most commonly, the eyes.

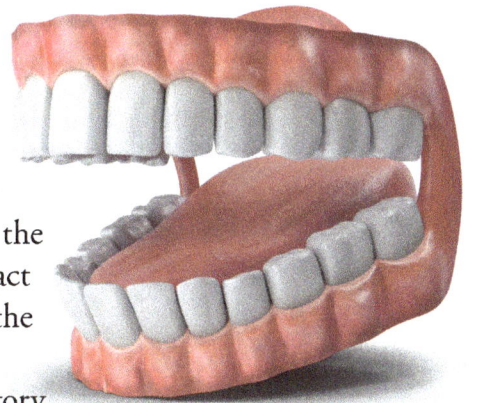

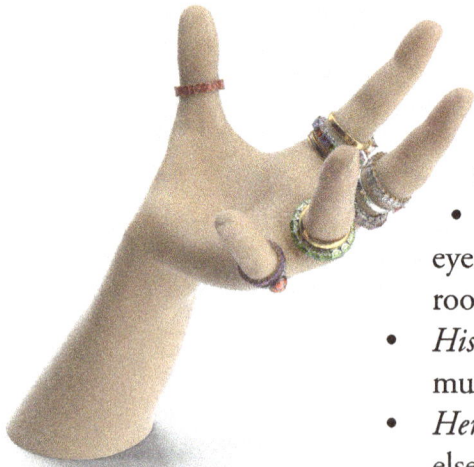

- *His eyes flew to hers.* (How far was that flight for his eyes and her eyes to meet up?)
- *Her eyes bounced around the room.* (Her eyes popped out of her head and bounced around the room, and no one noticed?)
- *His eyes followed the car down the street.* (What a sight that must be!)
- *Her eyes became angry.* (Did they have a fight with someone else's eyes?)

Eyes tend to crawl, roam, trail, bounce, and have emotions. The most common way to fix this is to use the word "gaze" in place of "eyes." Rewording your sentence or rethinking it entirely can also be very beneficial. For example, instead of "Her eyes became angry," try "She narrowed her eyes." It expresses the same idea, but the person is the one performing the action instead of the wandering body part.

Unfortunately, any body part can float.

- *His hand inched toward hers.*
- *Her jaw dropped to the floor.*
- *She gave him her hand.*
- *His face fell.*
- *Her head twisted.*

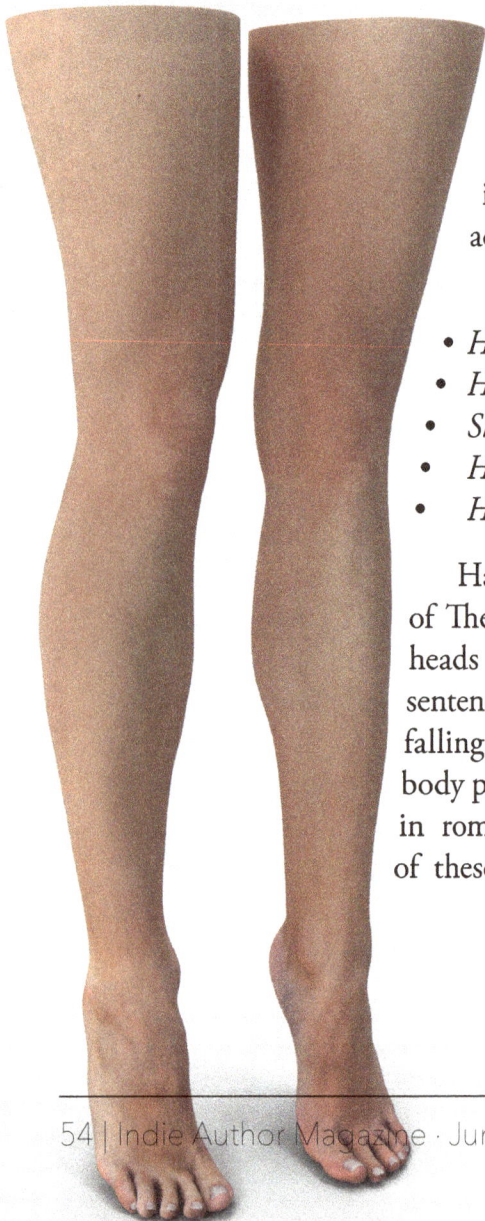

Hands doing things on their own is reminiscent of The Thing from *The Addams Family* while twisting heads is straight out of *The Exorcist*. Each of these sentences can be quickly restructured so that faces aren't falling off characters and people don't give away body parts, like their hearts—commonly found in romance novels. By imagining the visual of these sentences, you can easily catch your wandering body parts and put them back on the path to being attached to your character.

But are there any exceptions to the rule?

Yes, there are, just like with about any writing rule. The exception for wandering body parts is going to be your comfort level with writing them and whether your editor demands you reattach them. For instance, people roll their eyes. That's a common phrase in our everyday language. Readers won't hunt you down with pitchforks if a character rolls their eyes. Finding another way to express that character's displeasure, though, may just make you a better writer in the end.

If you enjoy comedy with your wandering body parts, there is no greater tale than the 1953 short story "The Eyes Have It" by Philip K. Dick. This masterpiece discusses body parts as if they are an alien life force. One especially amusing sentence is "Poor Bibney has lost his head again." Thankfully, this short story has been preserved in the public domain via Project Gutenberg (https://gutenberg.org/files/31516/31516-h/31516-h.htm).

Don't let wandering body parts frighten you or your readers. Carefully read the sentence with the body part and see if you can imagine the body part doing something on its own. If not, reword it. And remember, eyes cannot touch anyone physically. ■

Angela Martin

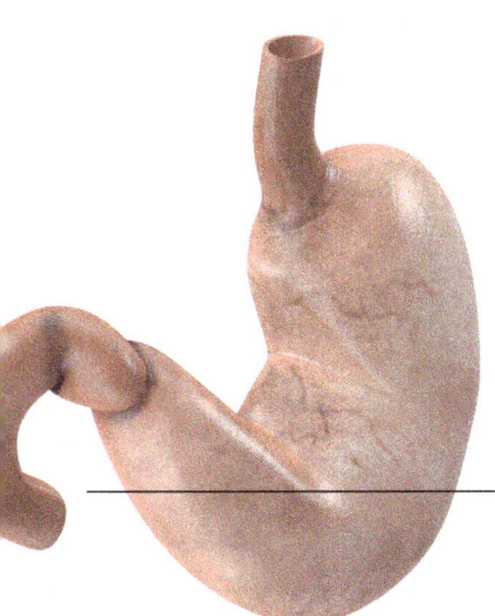

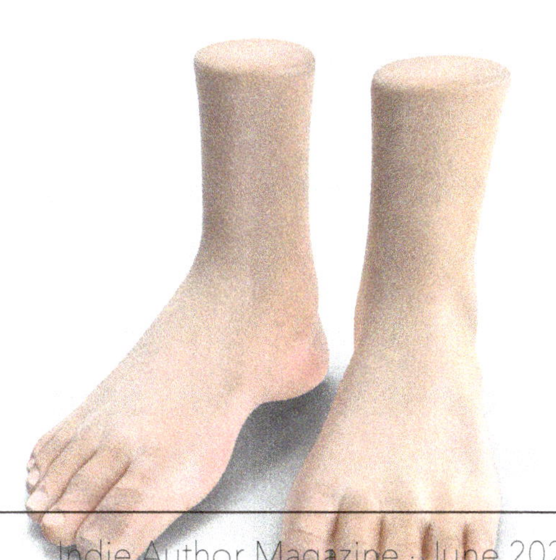

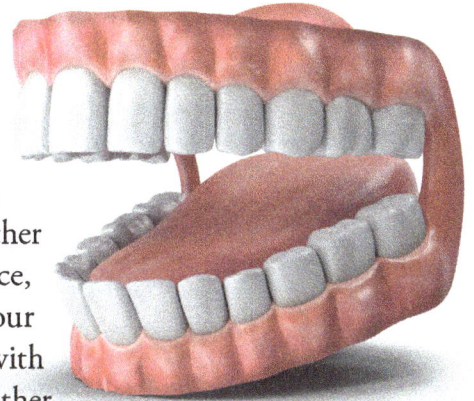

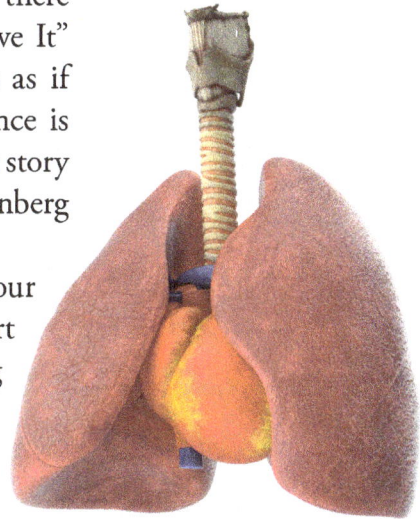

Season of the Witch

A CLOSER LOOK AT PARANORMAL WOMEN'S FICTION

The easiest definition of Paranormal Women's Fiction, or PWF as it's often referred to, is women's fiction with paranormal elements. More specifically, PWF is action-packed fiction under the fantasy umbrella written for and about women in the middle of their lives.

According to florasmusings.com, the genre is defined as "the new genre of paranormal romance (PNR), urban fantasy and paranormal cosy mystery stories where the female protagonists are Generation X," which seems to be a great starting point. A few solid examples from mainstream media might include the movies *Practical Magic*, *The Witches of Eastwick*, or even *Hocus Pocus* to some degree. And while all three of those examples are heavy on the standard "witch" trope, PWF stories are full of all varieties of paranormal and fantasy character types.

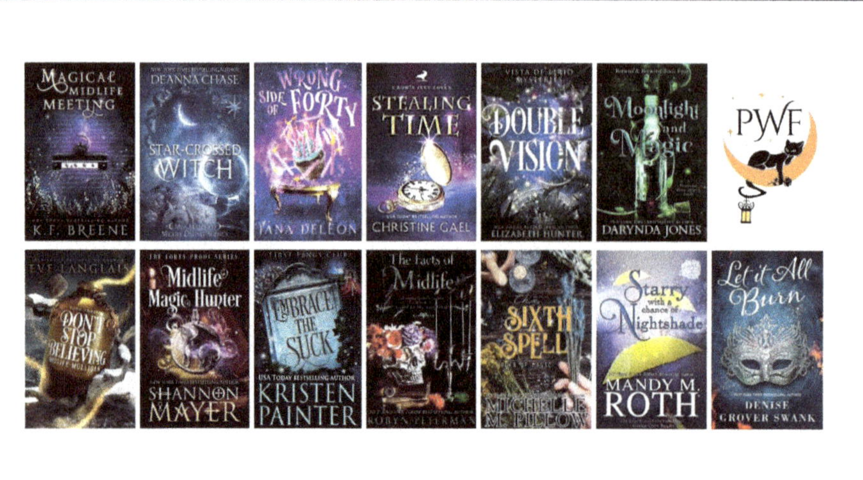

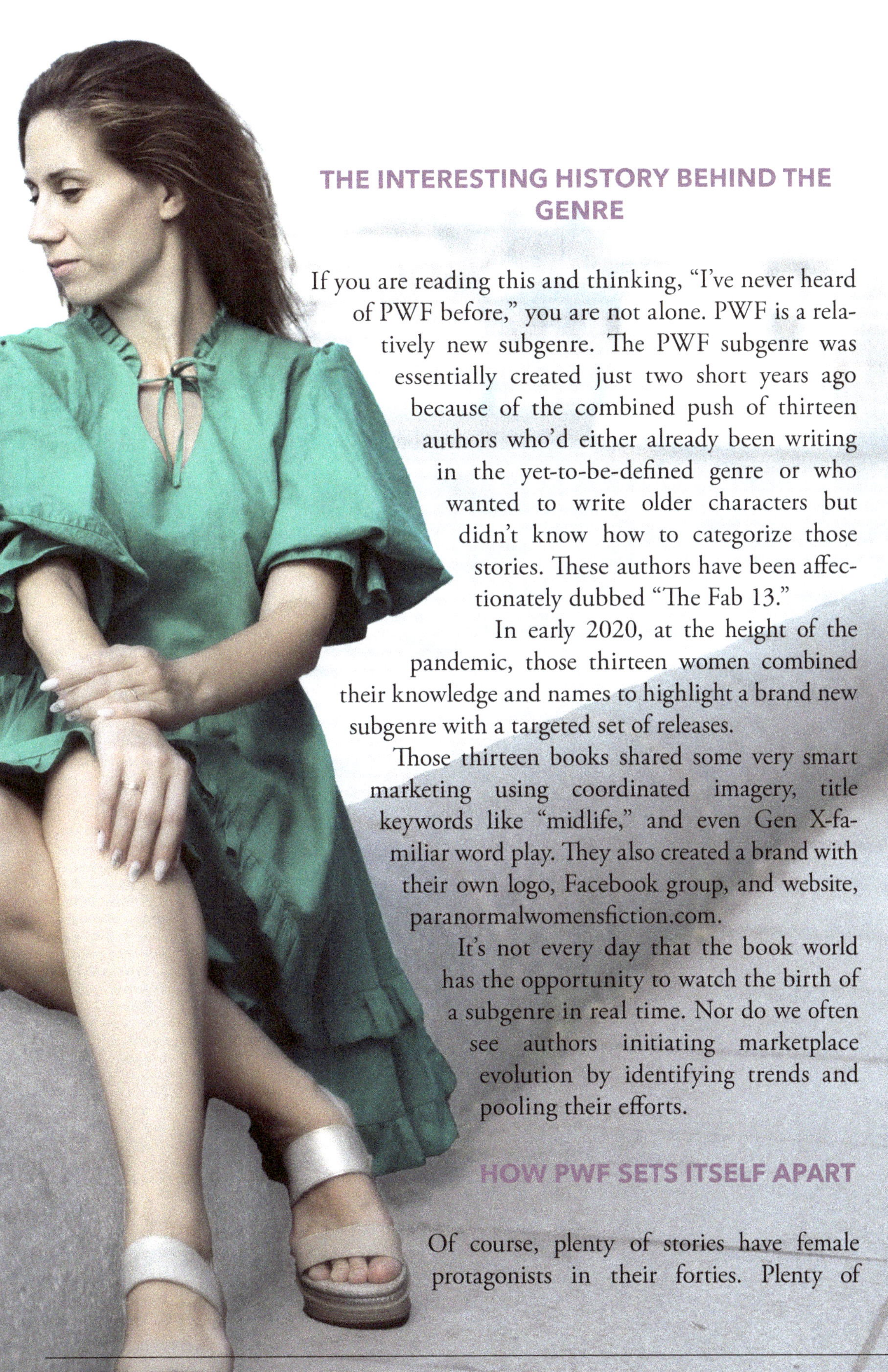

THE INTERESTING HISTORY BEHIND THE GENRE

If you are reading this and thinking, "I've never heard of PWF before," you are not alone. PWF is a relatively new subgenre. The PWF subgenre was essentially created just two short years ago because of the combined push of thirteen authors who'd either already been writing in the yet-to-be-defined genre or who wanted to write older characters but didn't know how to categorize those stories. These authors have been affectionately dubbed "The Fab 13."

In early 2020, at the height of the pandemic, those thirteen women combined their knowledge and names to highlight a brand new subgenre with a targeted set of releases.

Those thirteen books shared some very smart marketing using coordinated imagery, title keywords like "midlife," and even Gen X-familiar word play. They also created a brand with their own logo, Facebook group, and website, paranormalwomensfiction.com.

It's not every day that the book world has the opportunity to watch the birth of a subgenre in real time. Nor do we often see authors initiating marketplace evolution by identifying trends and pooling their efforts.

HOW PWF SETS ITSELF APART

Of course, plenty of stories have female protagonists in their forties. Plenty of mysteries even include paranormal elements and older characters. But until PWF began the process of defining itself, no category specifically existed for stories of magic and mystery with strong, competent, mature female protagonists dealing with exciting plots and real-life issues.

The local necromancer's teenage daughter just left for college, but she also has to stop an evil madman. The vegan vampire is in the middle of a divorce just before a mysterious magical event takes over her town. PWF makes it clear that even vampires and practitioners of the dark arts can experience tough times. Other examples of themes in PWF might include:

- grief over the death of a romantic partner or family member
- menopause
- health scares
- female friendships into adulthood
- dating after divorce
- raising children or teenagers
- relocation
- career change
- caring for elderly parents

Some of the above plot points might also be familiar in a genre like women's fiction, but the key is that these are fast-paced magical or paranormal stories more closely related to Urban Fantasy.

RESOURCES FOR WRITING PWF

If you've read this article and now think that Paranormal Women's Fiction might be relatable or a subgenre you'd like to try your hand at, more information is available—though maybe not to the extent that you can find in other subgenres.

For paid resources, the K-lytics report about PWF was updated in March 2022. You can find more about that here: https://k-lytics.com/paranormal-womens-fiction.

On the no-cost side, the PWF Facebook group is chock full of information, including guides and a guest author submission form. With a quick search, you can find several additional Facebook groups dedicated to this new subgenre for both readers and authors.

Currently, there is an active twitter thread at #paranormal-womensfiction, and Amazon has a public PWF book club (US only) and a FAB13 list.

What started as thirteen new releases has grown to include huge lists on Goodreads and targeted Amazon searches with enough magical material to keep you reading for years.

Now all you have to decide is if this developing genre has piqued your interest enough to research further, either as a reader or a writer. ■

Bre Loockhart

Writing with Chronic Illness

ONE AUTHOR'S ADVICE FOR FINDING BALANCE

Five years ago, author L.J. Stanton's future took a dramatic shift. An equestrian for much of her life, she'd earned an equine sciences degree in college and was training horses and teaching riding lessons for a living. Then she was diagnosed with two genetic disorders: Ehlers-Danlos syndrome (EDS) and postural orthostatic tachycardia syndrome (POTS).

"I didn't really look at it as anything serious until about five years ago with the diagnosis," she says. "And I realized that training horses and teaching riding lessons was just not feasible anymore, given my body."

After talking with her husband, she quit her job and turned to her other lifelong love: storytelling.

Stanton is one of countless authors with chronic illness who simultaneously manage their health and their writing careers. In 2018, the National Health Interview Survey (https://www.cdc.gov) found that more than half of US adults had at least one of ten chronic conditions, and more than 27 percent had more than one. Now, with many people experiencing lasting effects from COVID-19, more are learning to deal with long-term illness every day.

Stanton remembers having to make the same adjustment for herself. "I kind of understand what they're going through," she says, "because I felt like I was completely able-bodied, right up until basically the moment I wasn't." For her, finding a balance between her health and her writing means trying to push back against the "hustle culture" ingrained in the author industry. She tries to view productivity as progress toward a goal rather than reaching a certain word count, and she's made accommodations to her workspace to better suit her needs. But when she starts to push herself, her support system—her husband, her best friend, and her service dog, Chekov—offers the most help.

It's that support and sense of community she hopes other authors in her situation can find with one another through Reddit, Discord servers, or even writing conferences. Giving yourself space to grieve what you've lost after a new diagnosis is important, she says, but so is finding people who will help you afterward to focus on what you want to accomplish.

The work isn't just for those who have health conditions. Even authors without chronic illness can provide support to those who need it and improve disability and invisible illness representation through their books, something Stanton encourages.

"As authors, we have this really powerful medium for change," she says. "I think that if we see more of that included in writing, it is going to help people more who are now newly disabled and trying to navigate these really strange, uncomfortable waters." ■

Nicole Schroeder

Stability and Spikes

When your creative career is designed solely around stability, you may be tempted to resort to strict word counts, long hours, and crushing deadlines. That's a classic make-more-to-earn-more model. A creative career works best when it's diversified. Steady Eddie income—however small at first—is a worthy goal. But how do you make it grow?

Once you have your essential work on track, you can experiment until you get a spike. A spike can be big or small. It's any discovery that improves your process, your craft, and/or your marketing.

Last month, we streamlined your process with the four R's: Risk, Restlessness, Recycle, and Relinquish. You've identified your essential work and let go of the busy work. Now take the time you've rescued . . . and waste it on purpose. You use that remnant as a garden of inspiration and a lightning rod of creativity. You play. You grow as a writer and as an author.

Take time to forgive yourself. Reviewing your life and work with gratitude can revive hope and show you opportunities near at hand.

On the Creative Penn podcast, author David Kadavy talks about building stability and spikes into your creative career, "in part because having that stability helps you relax and relaxation is

what brings about insights. And then I try to spend the rest of my resources on . . . something that only I can do or . . . some idea that could be big. Probably won't, could be big."

He describes several massive spikes of success in his career, but Joanna Penn gives these words of encouragement: "I've never had a spike like that. So I would also encourage the audience. You don't have to have a spike . . . If you focus on producing your best creative work, then over time, you can make some kind of stability in terms of an income." ■

Laurel Decher

RESOURCES

Books

Productivity for Creative People by Mark McGuinness

Podcasts

"Mind Management, Not Time Management With David Kadavy" (The Creative Penn, April 26, 2021) https://www.thecreativepenn.com/2021/04/26/mind-management-not-time-management/

A Journalist's Guide to the Perfect Press Release

When it comes to press releases, I've worked on both sides of the writing desk. I've stared at the same blank page that other authors—or editorial interns, in my case—have tried to craft into an interest-grabbing announcement, just like I've sorted through stacks of those announcements in my email inbox to find the ones worth turning into a news story.

All that to say, I know how creating these short documents and making them effective can pose a challenge.

Press releases, at their most basic, are official statements sharing news or announcements with the media and other relevant organizations. Distributing them can often be done for free, and if they're successful, they have the ability to introduce you and your book to a number of potential new readers, often with a more personal connection than an advertisement.

Writing a press release well doesn't require mastery, but managing your own expectations and understanding the expectations your professional audience will carry about such announcements can help strengthen the chances that your news will be noticed. These basic tips are a solid place to start.

WHAT INFORMATION SHOULD YOU INCLUDE?

Newsrooms aren't quite the atmosphere of newsboy caps, rolled-up papers, and smoky office cubicles some might picture. But not every journalist stereotype deserves to end up on the cutting-room floor. That bustling, hectic newsroom? The writers who've perhaps

Press releases, at their most basic, are official statements sharing news or announcements with the media and other relevant organizations.

had one too many cups of coffee? At least in my experience, those are pretty accurate, so you need to pique interest quickly and keep your message to the point.

The best method for doing both of these is to put the most important information at the top, a journalistic story structure known as "the inverted pyramid," says Grace Halverson, an author and marketing communications specialist. "Often, to announce a new release, that will mean the title of your book and its release date, but other facts and information should be clearly defined as well," she says. These include the following:

- author name
- your contact information
- genre
- a brief description of the book
- a brief author bio
- high-resolution images of the book cover or your author photo (Note: Include these within the body of the release rather than as attachments)
- information on any events, such as book signings and/or author appearances
- other newsworthy information, such as books you've published, awards you've won, or reviews from well-known names

Press releases should be concise—about three hundred to four hundred words, writes journalist Janet Murray in a 2014 how-to guide on news releases published in *The Guardian*

Stick to the format of a press release, but let your press release's language mirror the tone and voice of your writing.

(https://theguardian.com)—and free of spelling or grammatical errors. They also should have a headline and either the words "for immediate release" or "embargoed until" the date you'd want the information made public, in bold and in all caps at the top.

"You would want it to be professional enough that you would be comfortable sending it to whoever you want to send it to, and they're going to take it seriously," Halverson says. "But at the same time, you can still be playful with your language within that." Stick to the format of a press release, but let your press release's language mirror the tone and voice of your writing.

WHERE SHOULD YOU SEND THEM?

Newspapers and magazines are some of the most common audiences for press releases, but they are far from the only options. "Try sharing your release with local independent bookstores, libraries, or book influencers to see if they're willing to repost your news on social media or in a newsletter," Halverson says. "The worst they can do is say, 'Oh, yeah, thanks. I don't know what we'll do with this.' But it's worth a shot." Submissions should be free to send to any local publication if done individually, she says—if there's a charge associated, the organization likely isn't legitimate. Third-party services also offer automatic wide distribution for a fee, but this option can be expensive and likely isn't the best alternative unless you're already an international bestseller, she notes.

No matter where you choose to distribute them, emailed press releases are generally preferred over snail mail, but use the format to your advantage. The subject line offers yet another chance to grab a journalist's attention, Halverson says, so make yours interesting and newsworthy. In the body of the email, write a short, personalized introductory message to whomever you're contacting, and paste the press release below that. Avoid attachments, according to Build Book Buzz (https://buildbookbuzz.com), as some people may be hesitant to open files from an unfamiliar source.

And be sure to do your research—sending your information to the wrong email address or to a staff member who wouldn't normally handle press releases could result in an automatic rejection. If you're unsure, ask someone in a separate email who to contact. The extra effort might even result in a better chance of the right person noticing your press release.

Above all, be sure your news is relevant to audiences you're trying to reach. Beyond local newspapers, magazines, or businesses, your book's release alone likely isn't worth a story, according to Creativindie (https://creativindie.com). Target your press releases carefully, and for larger publications, try to market your book indirectly through announcements that will appeal to a wider audience and will make your news unique and relevant.

WHAT KIND OF RESPONSE CAN YOU EXPECT?

Timing is key to generating action with your press release. Schedule emails for mid-mornings in the middle of the workweek, according to IssueWire (https://issuewire.com), a press release distribution site. Halverson agrees, saying authors should aim to send emails at least a week in advance, sometime between the start of the workday and lunch.

If you don't hear a response right away, it's also acceptable to try a second time. Wait a few days to a week after your original message, she says, then follow up.

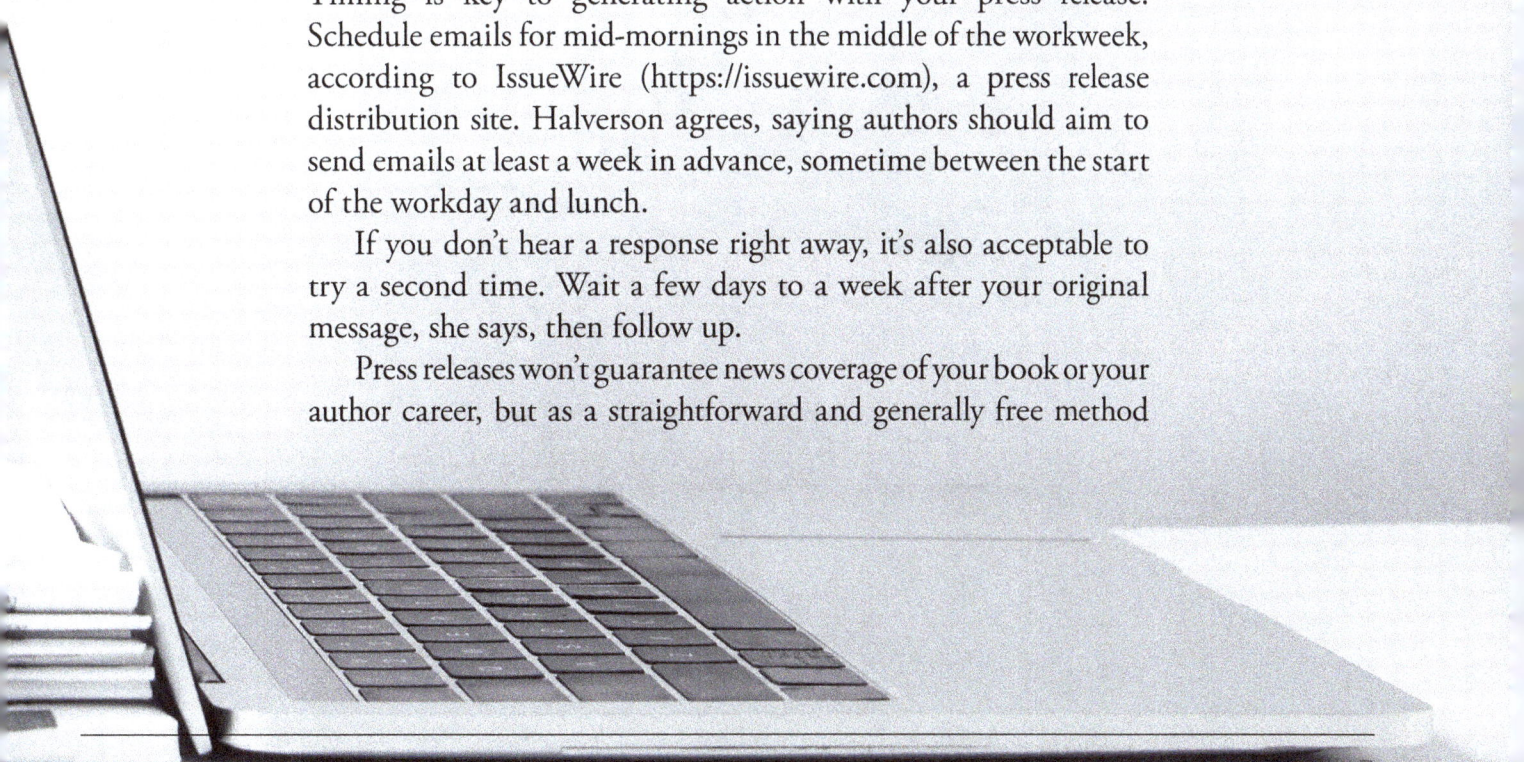

Press releases won't guarantee news coverage of your book or your author career, but as a straightforward and generally free method for garnering extra attention to your work, they're also easily overlooked. "Like querying, it's a numbers game," Halverson says. "Be prepared to send out a lot of them. And you know what? Sometimes all you need is one or two yeses.

"There is a line between obnoxious and persistent. Find it," she says. "Obviously, if they tell you to stop emailing them or they respond with a 'no,' don't push it, but if you're not getting responses, be friendly, but keep reaching out."

PRINT'S NOT DEAD

Still unsure how to structure your press release? Try using this example as a starting point. As you become more comfortable with the format over time, you'll be able to experiment with the language and voice to make it your own. ■

Nicole Schroeder

FOR IMMEDIATE RELEASE

Contact: John Smith, publisher@indieauthormagazine.com, (555) 123-4567

LOCAL AUTHOR TO PUBLISH 25TH NOVEL IN SEVEN YEARS

CITY, STATE (Date) — Something catchy. That's how Indie Author Magazine suggests you start your press release, and it's how local author John Smith has managed to enrapture readers for the past seven years with his independently published series of mystery novels, "The Armchair Detectives." Later this month, on May 30, Smith is set to publish his 25th novel and the final in the Armchair series, "The Writer Who Lost Her Words."

Set in sunny Bookland County, "The Writer Who Lost Her Words" follows everyone's favorite detective, Hugh Dunnit, as he works to tie off the last dangling thread of his illustrious career before retirement: the disappearance of bestselling writer Jane Doe's manuscript — and of Jane Doe herself. Hugh only has one month left before he turns in his badge, but when he discovers a clue to Jane's whereabouts in a set of old files, the case is turned on its head. Could Hugh have been overlooking the answer this whole time? And will his deduction skills be enough to uncover the answer to the biggest mystery he's ever faced before he leaves the field forever?

"The Writer Who Lost Her Words" will be available on Kindle and Barnes & Noble platforms in both e-book and paperback formats. Smith's books have sold nearly 1 million copies since the series debut, with his most recent book launching him into the top-50 spot in Amazon's bestseller charts for his genre.

"It's bittersweet to say goodbye to these characters, but I hope the readers are as enthralled in this last mystery as I was writing it," Smith said.

A lifelong resident of CITY, Smith's love of writing was rivaled only by his love of detective shows. After he'd exhausted the library of its mystery novels, and at the insistence of his high school English teacher, he began writing his own. Now, the biggest mystery is how he manages to keep up with all the story ideas in his head.

To celebrate his book's launch, Smith will be selling signed copies at the farmers market on Friday, June 3.

For more information or to arrange an interview, please contact:
John Smith, author, publisher@indieauthormagazine.com, (555) 123-4567

###

From the Stacks

Courtesy of IndieAuthorTools.com
Got a book you love and want to share with us?
Submit a book at IndieAuthorTools.com

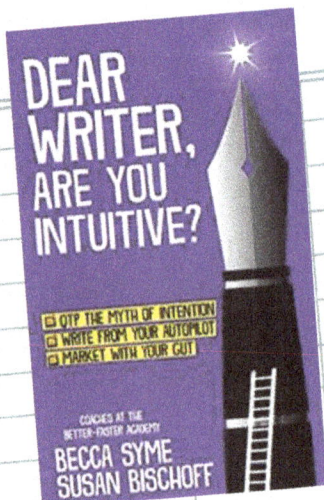

Dear Writer, Are You Intuitive?

https://books2read.com/u/bo2pDp

Dear Writer, Are You Intuitive? celebrates differences. "In our work coaching writers," co-author Becca Syme says, "we see so many people who feel pressured to explain (or explain away) their intuition. They feel they need to be more concrete and more linear, rather than embracing the intuitive self. Our goal in this book is to deconstruct intuition a little, provide some guidance about care and feeding, and then give some tips and tools to grow and guide that intuitive self in all parts of your career."

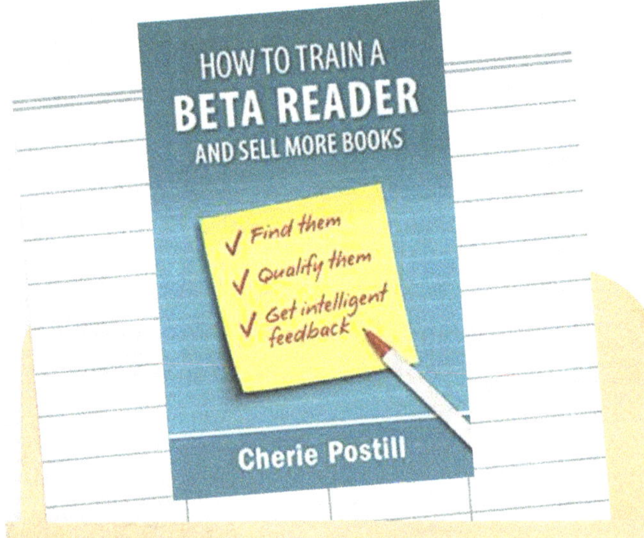

How to Train a Beta Reader and Sell More Books

https://books2read.com/u/md6jnX

Take the mystery out of the beta testing process with How to Train a Beta Reader and Sell More Books. When done correctly, beta testing your manuscript helps you produce your best work and attract additional readers. This concise guide was written by Cherie Postill, author and veteran marketing professional. It contains a wealth of actionable advice as well as access to a template you can use to create a customized beta reader questionnaire.

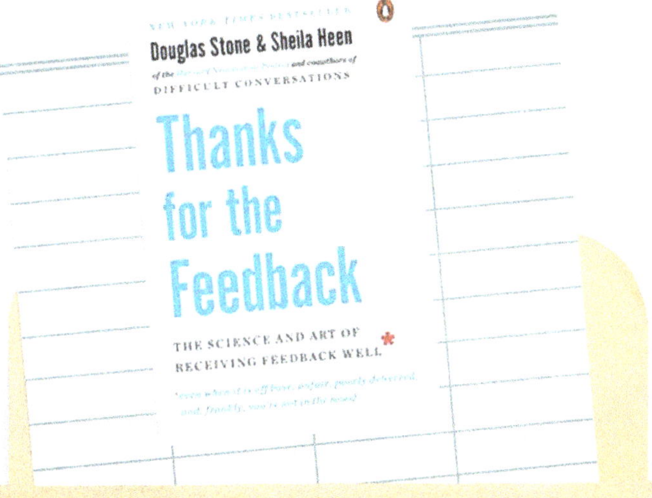

Thanks for the Feedback: The Science and Art of Receiving Feedback Well
https://books2read.com/u/3n5D8B
Audiobook available
This communication skills book focuses on the giving and taking of feedback. Business consultants Douglas Stone and Sheila Heen make a case for adopting a growth mindset in order to get the most out of this frequently misinterpreted process. Thanks for the Feedback contains helpful examples and practical tips along with pertinent findings from psychology and neuroscience.

Cover to Cover: What First-Time Authors Need to Know about Editing
https://books2read.com/u/4jg5LY
Audiobook available
Wondering if you should work with an editor or beta readers? Sandra Wendel's guide - Cover to Cover: What First-Time Authors Need to Know about Editing - answers that and many more questions frequently posed by newbie and aspiring authors. Take some of the mystery out of the book production process with this humorous, straightforward book.

Productivity for Creative People
https://books2read.com/u/bz1Kgq
Learn how to carve out time for your most important creative work in Productivity for Creative People: How to Get Creative Work Done in an "Always On" World. In this concise book, Mark McGuinness offers practical strategies for dealing with the distractions of daily life that can derail our writing. These tips, techniques, and insights are gleaned from his practice as a poet, nonfiction writer, and coach of creative individuals.

In This Issue

Executive Team

Chelle Honiker, Publisher

As the publisher of Indie Author Magazine, Chelle Honiker brings nearly three decades of startup, technology, training, and executive leadership experience to the role. She's a serial entrepreneur, founding and selling multiple successful companies including a training development company, travel agency, website design and hosting firm, a digital marketing consultancy, and a wedding planning firm. She's organized and curated multiple TEDx events and hired to assist other nonprofit organizations as a fractional executive, including The Travel Institute and The Freelance Association.

As a writer, speaker, and trainer she believes in the power of words and their ability to heal, inspire, incite, and motivate. Her greatest inspiration is her daughters, Kelsea and Cathryn, who tolerate her tendency to run away from home to play with her friends around the world for months at a time. It's said she could run a small country with just the contents of her backpack.

Alice Briggs, Creative Director

As the creative director of Indie Author Magazine, Alice Briggs utilizes her more than three decades of artistic exploration and expression, business startup adventures, and leadership skills. A serial entrepreneur, she has started several successful businesses. She brings her experience in creative direction, magazine layout and design, and graphic design in and outside of the indie author community to her role.

With a masters of science in Occupational Therapy, she has a broad skill set and uses it to assist others in achieving their desired goals. As a writer, teacher, healer, and artist, she loves to see people accomplish all they desire. She's excited to see how IAM will encourage many authors to succeed in whatever way they choose. She hopes to meet many of you in various places around the world once her passport is back in use.

Writers

Bradley Charbonneau

Bradley Charbonneau wanted to be a writer. Trouble was, he didn't write. A friend was running a "Monthly Experiment" (no coffee for a month, wake up at 5 AM, etc.) and created one where everyone had to write every single day for 30 days. Bradley took the challenge. "Hmm, that wasn't so bad." Then he kept going. 100 days. 365. 1,000. 2,808 days and 31 books later and he found out it's simple. Not necessarily easy, but simple. #write #everysingleday

Laurel Decher

There might be no frigate like a book, but publishing can feel like a voyage on the H.M.S. Surprise. There's always a twist and there's never a moment to lose.

Laurel's mission is to help you make the most of today's opportunities. She's a strategic problem-solver, tool collector, and co-inventor of the "you never know" theory of publishing.

As an epidemiologist, she studied factors that help babies and toddlers thrive. Now she writes books for children ages nine to twelve about finding more magic in life. She's a member of the Society for Children's Book Writers and Illustrators (SCBWI), has various advanced degrees, and a tendency to smuggle vegetables into storylines.

Fatima Fayez

As a writer for Indie Author Magazine, Fatima unites her love of connecting with people and giving back to the author community. She is a co-founder of The Author Arena podcast, in addition to The Author Conference on Clubhouse. She is also an administrator for the 20BooksTo50K® Facebook group.

Fatima has lived in countries across Europe, Asia, and North America. During her various residencies, she managed to collect a bachelor of science in Journalism, along with a masters in Business Administration, and a handful of management certifications. She currently resides in Kuwait with her family.

On Saturdays, you can find her playing Dungeons & Dragons with her party.

Gill Fernley

Gill Fernley writes fiction in several genres under different pen names, but what all of them have in common is humour and romance, because she can't resist a happy ending or a good laugh. She's also a freelance content writer and has been running her own business since 2013. Before that, she was a technical author and documentation manager for an engineering company and can describe to you more than you'd ever wish to know about airflow and filtration in downflow booths. Still awake? Wow, that's a first! Anyway, that experience taught her how to explain complex things in straightforward language and she hopes it will come in handy for writing articles for IAM. Outside of writing, she's a cake decorator, expert shoe hoarder, and is fluent in English, dry humour and procrastibaking.

Chrishaun Keller-Hanna

Chrishaun Keller-Hanna is an award-winning journalist, teacher, technical writer, and fiction author that lives for explaining difficult concepts in a way that non-technical readers can understand.

She spent twenty years teaching literacy and composition to a variety of students from kindergarten to college level and writing technical documentation for several tech companies in the Austin area. At the age of forty-three, she decided to write fiction and has published over thirty titles so far with plans to extend out to comics and board games.

When she's not writing, she's traveling, playing video games, or watching movies. When she's not doing THAT, she's talking about them with her husband and grown daughters.

Kasia Lasinska

Kasia Lasinska holds an LLB in Law with European Legal Studies and an LL.M. in Advanced Studies in International Law. As a practicing attorney, Kasia worked with a top international human rights barrister and then advised clients at a large, international law firm. These inspired her to write dystopian and fantasy novels about corrupt governments and teenagers saving the world.

Kasia has lived in eight countries and speaks five languages (fluently after a glass of wine). She currently lives in London, but her daydreams are filled with beaches and palm trees.

When she's not writing, you can find Kasia scouting out the best coffee shops in town, planning her next great adventure, or petting other people's puppies.

Bre Lockhart

Armed with a degree in Communications and Public Relations, Bre Lockhart survived more than a decade in the corporate America trenches before jumping headfirst into writing urban fantasy and sci-fi, followed later by mystery under a second pen name. She's also one-third of a fiction editing team who probably enjoy their jobs a bit too much most days. As an experienced extrovert, Bre uses her questionable humor and red—sometimes other colors, too—glasses at writer conferences to draw unsuspecting introverts into her bubble of conversation; no one is safe. On her days off, you can find Bre camping and traveling with her family or organizing an expansive collection of lipstick at her home in Tulsa, Oklahoma.

Angie Martin

Award-winning author Angie Martin has spent over a decade mentoring and helping new and experienced authors as they prepare to send their babies into the world. She relies on her criminal justice background and knack for researching the tiniest of details to assist others when crafting their own novels. She has given countless speeches in various aspects of writing, including creating characters, self-publishing, and writing supernatural and paranormal. She also assisted in leading a popular California writers' group, which organized several book signings for local authors. In addition to having experience in film, she created the first interactive murder mystery on Clubhouse and writes and directs each episode. Angie now resides in rural Tennessee, where she continues to help authors around the world in every stage of publication while writing her own thriller and horror books, as well as branching out into new genres.

Susan Odev

Susan has banked over three decades of work experience in the fields of personal and organizational development, being a freelance corporate trainer and consultant alongside holding down "real" jobs for over twenty-five years. Specializing in entrepreneurial mindsets, she has written several non-fiction business books, once gaining a coveted Amazon #1 best seller tag in business and entrepreneurship, an accolade she now strives to emulate with her fiction.

Currently working on her fifth novel, under a top secret pen name, the craft and marketing aspects of being a successful indie author equally fascinate and terrify her.

A lover of history with a criminal record collection, Susan lives in a retro orange and avocado world. Once described by a colleague as being an "onion," Susan has many layers, as have ogres (according to Shrek). She would like to think this makes her cool, her teenage children just think she's embarrassing.

Nicole Schroeder

Nicole is a storyteller at heart. A journalist, author, and editor from Columbia, Missouri, she delights in any opportunity to shape her own stories or help others do the same. Graduating with a bachelor's degree from the Missouri School of Journalism and minors in English and Spanish, she's worked as a copyeditor for a small-town newspaper and as an editor for a local arts and culture magazine. Her creative writing has been published in national literary magazines, and she's helped edit numerous fiction and nonfiction books, including a Holocaust survivor's memoir, alongside international independent publishers. When she's not at her writing desk, Nicole is usually in the saddle, cuddling her guinea pigs, or spending time with family. She loves any excuse to talk about Marvel movies and considers National Novel Writing Month its own holiday.

INDIE AUTHOR MAGAZINE
INDIE AUTHOR MAGAZINE

COME VISIT
the Cake Machine
STAY for the Conference.
Las Vegas
Nevada
November
14-18, 2022
writelink.to/20Books
20BOOKS TO 50K®
A RISING TIDE LIFTS ALL BOATS

www.ingramcontent.com/pod-product-compliance
Lightning Source LLC
Chambersburg PA
CBHW081747200326
41597CB00024B/4421
* 9 7 8 1 9 5 7 1 1 8 0 6 2 *